ETERNAL

Autobiography of

Gladstone Matthew

Order this book online at www.trafford.com
or email orders@trafford.com

Most Trafford titles are also available at major online book retailers.

Printed in the United States of America.

ISBN: 978-1-4269-6753-5 (sc)
ISBN: 978-1-4269-6754-2 (e)

Trafford rev. 12/22/2011

 www.trafford.com

North America & international
toll-free: 1 888 232 4444 (USA & Canada)
phone: 250 383 6864 ♦ fax: 812 355 4082

CHAPTER 1

In the beginning there was love. I was suffering from bronchitis at the age of four and my grandmother Miss Cochrane was there for me. She was in her late fifties. Miss Cochrane made her own remedies to make me well from roots found in the hills of Johnson's Point, a small village in Antigua of the West Indies. She would put plaster on my chest, which was a strange type of sticky hot cloth. There were times when she would carry me in her arms to Doctor King's office on the hill in Johnson's Point. At that time the doctor didn't know what was wrong or what to do. It was a frightening time in the beginning.

At nights when I was sick I would lie on top of her while trying to sleep. Her eyes were full of grief and fear. I survived and her love made me well. It had been like I was going to die and there was nothing anyone could do. I became the favourite, her little Baba. Anytime I wanted a hug she was there. She was always sitting on the front steps of the house while watching her grandchildren in the yard.

Bruce was the oldest and my cousin. Miss Cochrane was rough at times with Bruce. She would say, "You are the ringleader." One evening I saw her sitting on Bruce. He was seven years old at the time when I saw that. Bruce was crying out for help, but somehow I knew that she was love. Denise was the second oldest and my sister. She was like a tomboy growing up with three boys. Leslie was the youngest and Bruce's brother; anywhere I was, he was.

Antigua was a small Island of 108 square miles in the Atlantic Ocean. In Antigua of the West Indies the warm wind from the dry season would blow on the mango trees in the yard. The rainy season brought the high winds over the roaring sea and the fear of a hurricane was always. The cock would crow in the morning with the rising of the sun shining bright over the mountains and the sky bright blue.

The four of us knew each other when we were children. We were too young to understand how we ended up living with Miss Cochrane, but where were our parents? My grandmother would say something to me like this, "Your uncle came back from England and he brought with him some clothes and shoes from your mother." She didn't say much about my mother, which I do remember. Miss Cochrane was the one who nurtured us in the beginning. There was no life before her in my mind at that time.

When Denise and I were four and five, we would visit Bolans village in Antigua some weekends. Our father's parents lived there. We called them Mommy and Daddy. Bolans was west of Johnson's Point and the scenery was quite vibrant. There was a huge pasture right across the road from my grandparent's house. Out there was where my grandfather raised cattle, and beyond that we could see the cane fields.

Bolans School was right across the street on the east side of the house facing south. The house was situated too close to the road and was painted beige. Bingo the dog was out there to play with. Inside, the house was very modest with wooden chairs and oil lamps. There was no electricity or running water in the house, but there was a water pipe down the road east of the house where the villagers would take their buckets to fetch water for cooking and bathing.

My grandfather's name was Dan Matthew, and he was the most respected man in Bolans. I had the most fun in Bolans.

The house in Johnson's Point was painted white and was facing the south road. The outhouse was west of the house beyond the trees near to the fence. The kitchen was separated from the house. Les and I played on the concrete steps by the house. We played there most of the time. The house had two bedrooms and three of us slept with Miss Cochrane. Unfortunately Les was a bed wetter. Bruce slept in the other bedroom with our aunt. The sleeping condition for six years was awful.

My sister and I fought a lot when we were kids. Bruce and Les were brothers, and there was no friction between the three of us.

The beginning of my life was a mystery. There was never a time that I can remember before Johnson's Point. But there was another time in London England. It was a short time especially for Denise and me.

We were taught not to keep people company. Miss Cochrane didn't have many friends. The neighbour's children were not allowed in the yard. It was an awkward time. However, her values were straightforward. I treasure some of those values today.

Miss Cochrane was born in Saint Johns, Antigua west of Johnson's Point. She had long black hair with Asian features. She became an orphan after her mother died. Her father was of mixed race with long black hair. He worked at the theatre.

At times before going to town she would lock us up in the kitchen with a basket lunch. She trusted no one with her grandchildren. The boy next door was not allowed to communicate with us from the other side of the fence, and we had to be in pairs on our way back home every time.

Johnson's Point was where I began to remember my tragic beginning. Miss Cochrane never had a man around the house. We were growing up with a disciplinarian who nurtured our lives.

On the weekends Matilda would visit us bringing with her magazines to read and lots of sweets. She was tall and slender.

Also, I do remember when the dog fell down the hole in the outhouse and somehow Miss Cochrane used a stick to fetch him out. It was a smelly situation.

One night I dashed across the street to follow Miss Cochrane. Then I fell awkwardly by the wheel of a car. Miss Cochrane dropped the basket that was on her head while quickly looking back at the car coming to a halt. My aunt told me that it was not a dream. I almost got run over by a car. It was a close call. My eyes were looking straight at the wheel of the car. A lot of strange things happened in Johnson's Point.

I was afraid of everything; that's how I was being raised. Miss Cochrane was extremely over protective. Somehow school was where we had a little freedom. Sometimes I felt isolated in the yard even though I had Les to play with.

I remember the time when Les got cut on the back of his head by a shoe heel thrown by the boy next door. Les did not cry even though there was blood. Miss Cochrane went after the boy with great anger saying, "That's what happens when you keep people company." Les was a tough kid with a bad temper.

Miss Cochrane was brutal at times. I saw her throw a stone at my aunt's face; the result was a busted lip. Tears came down my aunt's face while Miss Cochrane stood there ready for a fight. Miss Cochrane was a troubled soul. However, I loved her more than anything.

Miss Cochrane had fights with her sister-in-law at the fence. They would throw buckets of water on each other and use awful language. She had a troubled childhood. Her father was not there. Her husband, Stanley Cochrane, abandoned her and his children. She became very bitter toward the world.

Miss Cochrane's oldest son was Uncle Bong. Uncle Eustace was the second followed by Sonia, my mother. Aunt Doris was the youngest. Johnson's Point was my foundation and innocence. It was there where my tears were dried.

There was a very tragic day that day should never had happened. That day was when I met my father. It was the beginning of hardships for me. Miss Cochrane told me that my father was coming to Johnson's Point to take me to Toronto. There was no joy in my heart. I was eight years old at the time.

My father was a stranger in the yard. I never had a father in my life. He was built like Charles Atlas and very uncomfortable looking. He wasn't comfortable when I was sitting on his lap in the house. There were no hugs. He paid no attention to me and I felt it. My father never existed at all even though I saw him walking through the gate.

My sister was running away from him. However, he was very affectionate with her. There was laughter with her that I remember. I was left out of the celebration, which was painful. He never loved me. From the beginning there was isolation and rejection. I wanted the same treatment that my sister was getting with the same laughter. My father loved his daughter. Making me happy was what I had to do.

Before we left for Toronto, my sister threw a stone at me cutting my left toe. I bear a scar there to this day. I was walking with a limp on the airplane.

Bruce and Les were also coming to Toronto. It was time to leave Johnson's Point. It was December 10, 1968. Miss Cochrane was my only hope and protection.

Toronto, Canada was a very cold city. It was always warm in Johnson's Point with the wind blowing over the mountains and the sound of nature with the singing of birds.

There were so many people in Toronto. It was intimidating. Canadians spoke English but it was difficult at times to understand their accent. Many lights were shining in the night. The roads were long and wide, and there were many cars. Toronto was a different style of life, but it didn't take me too long to forget Johnson's Point.

I met my mother for the first time, and I remember my mother saying that I was a dunce. She was sitting on the bed in her nightgown. I got a hug from her, but it was not what I expected. There was no love. She was not the mother that I wanted and I knew that right away. I was the child with no hope. For sure, I had a mountain to climb.

It was tough mentally on the four of us. Toronto was a complicated scene. There was so much bubble gum to chew in Toronto. It would have been better for me if Miss Cochrane was in Toronto. Life was a disaster with my parents. The feeling of rejection was in my heart.

We lived on Bloor Street. The houses were old and gray and attached. The neighborhood was clean and quiet. There was nothing to do in the morning. We were not going to school, so we watched television every day. The game of hockey was on television and I loved it right away. The Toronto Maple Leafs was my favourite hockey team.

Loneliness was the feeling I had being around my father. Anyway, it was time to move on to a new home. Bruce and Les came with us but their stay was short. It was the beginning of grief and many awful things. The climate was good and my bronchitis was gone.

CHAPTER 2

Lynngate School was the place where part of my heart will be always. I got my wisdom from the game of baseball in that neighbourhood. It was a privilege being a kid in 1969. I went searching for Lynngate School on my bicycle and my heart was pounding in anticipation of what I would find. Nothing has changed in my old neighbourhood. The big sign that says Lynngate Park was still there. The swings on the east side of the School were rusty and gray but nevertheless still standing. On the right side of the swings, looking through a path, you could see a softball diamond, and that's where Lynda Russell was a star.

A huge soccer field was at the back of the school. The children played soccer every recess and the matches were competitive. Running down the hill with the soccer ball in my hand, I was a young boy with bubblegum spit in my mouth. It was frantic on the soccer field with the screaming and hollering, "Chris, pass the ball, stop hogging the ball, Mike." That was the scene on the soccer field at recess time.

I remember falling down and hitting my head on the pavement at the back of the school, and that's where I was standing on this day.

The school was haunted by childhood memories. I felt so much hurt. On the wall inside of the school, I saw a picture of Denise in her softball uniform. She was ten years old and smiling in the picture with her teammates. Her accomplishments on the softball field were great. Lynngate won the pennant in softball for the first time when my sister and I were there. Being a winner brought tears of joy on my sister's face and the feeling of joy in her heart after the final out was made to win the softball championship.

My childhood days were full of drama. At school, I dominated in track and field. We were the champions of hope. I was a part of the thrill and triumph on the softball field.

However, I never went to a sporting event with my father. Sporting events were supposed to bring father and son together. My father and I were never close. I can't remember ever seeing him in my bedroom. His heart was too hard. This man was invisible from my youth. I was like a defenseless boxer in the corner of the room when my father was home. The tension in my heart would mount.

"Dad, let's go to the ball park," that was my friend David talking to his father. David and his father were playing catch and I wanted to play. I was happy playing softball even though my father was not there. From the sidelines I would see fathers and sons holding hands. "Come on son, put a little bit more power in your swing," that's how a father would talk at the ball park. "How was that swing dad?" "That's great, son. I am proud of you. Now let's play catch." Love was what it was all about on the playing fields with David and his father.

At times I would look to the ground and wonder why my father was so mean to me. He was the problem in my young life. My father never said that he was proud of me. In Johnson's Point, Miss Cochrane was like a father.

My father took me to buy winter boots and that was the only time I can remember ever going anywhere with him. He became angry while I was trying on a pair of boots that were too tight. "What are you doing, boy? Can't you see that the shoe is too tight?" He looked at me while dragging the boot from my foot. It was an impossible situation.

We lived at 50 Tourmaline Drive in a beautiful semi— detached house. What I remember most about that house was that I had to walk up some stairs to get to my parents' bedroom. We had a beautiful black-and-white television set which sat between beautiful red curtains. The back yard was fenced-in. There was a fence right across the street facing south, and beyond that the bushes and the 401 Highway that ran east and west. White people in the neighbourhood surrounded us on all sides but that was never a problem. It was rare to find black people in Scarborough around the late 1960s.

For the first time I saw snow while looking through the windows at school. The snowflakes were falling and disappearing on the ground very quickly. I had no idea of what was happening. The afternoon school bell would take forever to ring while my mind was on baseball and bubblegum cards.

It was a terrible situation with my father, but I tried to cope with a broken heart at home. No one was there to show me how to play the game of baseball. My father was supposed to be my best friend. At that time, my father had a mean spirit.

I lived in a home without love. It was silent most of the time. I desperately needed to find something of joy to keep me going. My childhood days with my father were very bitter and out-of-phase. And I was struggling with my personality. My only hopes were hockey cards and baseball cards, especially baseball. Babe Ruth made the game of baseball so romantic. I was fascinated with the intrigue and the history of the game of baseball. Baseball was deep and tragic for heroes like Jackie Robinson. Baseball was my other world.

I created my own simulated hockey game with hockey cards and the bedroom floor was the sporting arena. I would scream, "Keon shoots, he scores!" I was too loud and so alone. The hockey cards were alive in my mind. It was quite interesting the way I was behaving in my bedroom with my bubblegum cards. My heart was with the Toronto Maple Leafs hockey team and bubblegum cards even though the New York Mets baseball cards were my favourite. The New York Mets made dreams come true.

My hockey hero was Maple Leafs captain Dave Keon. He was great theatre on ice like a ballerina he could play hockey, but he was playing for a lousy team. Keon would have scored 600 goals if he had played for the Montreal Canadians. He would have been considered the greatest Canadian ever.

When I was nine years old I knew how to skate and handle the puck at the school rink. I loved the game of hockey then but not now. Too much coaching has destroyed the creativity of the game. Let the players play the game with their God-given imagination. Too much emphasis is wasted on the strategy of how to play the game without the puck, and the players shoot the puck in too often from the blue line. Also, the street hockey mentality is gone from the game. Only one coach is needed behind the bench. Trying to teach Bobby Orr how to play hockey without the puck today would be insane. Bobby Orr always had the puck and he was playing defense.

No one was there to guide me at home. My feelings and thoughts about that time were too tragic. My heart did hurt too much when looking for love from my parents. My father didn't want to understand my wants and needs. The world was laughing at me, and I was in pain and suffering internally when I was looking for my father. I was withdrawing slowly from the world which was dangerous. My parents took better care of their friends and relatives at 50 Tourmaline Drive. My sister and I were the outsiders. The four of us never sat together as a family around the dinner table.

Collecting baseball cards was exciting for me without a father. The struggle with my father was unusual with more pain on the way. At night my mind was preoccupied with baseball heroes like Chicago Cubs Billy Williams.

School was mentally tough at times with so much uncertainty at home. I remember failing grade three and crying in front of my classmates. My teachers never ever met my parents. My parents didn't care about my education. I was nine years old and trapped in a bedroom with my thoughts.

The 1969, New York Mets was a special baseball moment in time. Cleon Jones made the final out and the Angeles jumped for joy. This was a baseball miracle. The timing was magical with man walking on the moon. The Mets won the World Series for the ages. It was so awesome watching those dramatic catches in the outfield by Ron Swoboda and Tommie Agee. Tommie Agee was the World Series.

I had hundreds of baseball cards in my room. I was being laughed at. "Why are you wasting your money on baseball cards, are they worth anything?" My sister would say that all the time, "Are you crazy?" Nothing was more important than bubblegum cards. My bedroom was like Cooperstown.

I was afraid and uncomfortable when I was sick at home one day. The curtains moved and there was a haunting presence in the house. Right away I started talking to myself, "Is someone in the house? Who is there?" I called my aunt and said, "Auntie, someone is in the house." She said, "Who is in the house?" My aunt was startled. "Auntie, I don't know." "Look, if you are scared go next door." Later that evening my mother jokingly said that my grandfather came to visit me that afternoon. My mother's father died before I was born. No one had a logical explanation for what happened to me when the curtains moved in the house. My mind was not there that afternoon; that was a provoking time.

I played simulated baseball games with my bubblegum cards. No father was there to show me how to play the game of life, which was the most important thing. The "black-

and-white" filmstrips of the 1927 New York Yankees were awesome and impressionable. I loved the Babe and the Iron Horse Lou Gehrig. My mind will always be trapped in that frame of thinking. The courage to stand up to my father was not there. My father never existed it seemed, so daydreaming was my only hope in my bizarre childhood.

No mother was there to give me love. I was on my own. My mother was a great failure. My father was the same. They were without responsibility.

Hockey and baseball gave me that slim hope of believing in the impossible. My schoolwork was in jeopardy and it was hard to concentrate in the classroom with other things on my mind. I was becoming a baseball encyclopedia in the loneliness of my bedroom. My happiness was being ruined by my father. Time stood still for the children who were not guided in the right direction. The potential I had to become a great athlete was never reached.

My father had the wrong attitude around his own son. Empty was the way my father was at home. There was no chance to become father and son. It was that way all the time.

My father and sister had some communication. In the wintertime they shoveled snow off the driveway together with laughter. He loved her but he was never there for her either.

My father liked to dress up in three-piece suits to show the world that he was something. The rumour was that he had a girlfriend on the side. Whatever, my mother was not bothered with things like that. Every night my mother would be on the phone in her nightgown. She was in her own world.

I was hurt when my father refused to pick up my simulated baseball board game from the post office. Eventually, the game was shipped back to the United States. "Your father said that it was a waste of money," that's what my mother told me. I dreamed about that game every night. And it was painful to let that go. No love was there between father and son.

At that time I became a hero for the day on the softball field. I was daydreaming with my softball glove in my hand. Then a softball was hit straight at me and my only reaction was to catch the ball without my glove. It was an incredible catch to win the ball game. All the parents jumped and cheered. My teammates hugged me; that moment was sweet. David's father, Mr. Berry, was there. Willie Mays would have been proud of me.

After the celebration, I was in shock. It was great though. I had a smile on my face but my father wasn't there. The applause I got at that moment was not coming from my father. Mr. Berry who was there for his son drove me home. He told my father, "Your son made a great catch." My father said, "very good" with a smile. He did not say that he was proud of me or, "Let's go for some ice cream." I stood there feeling out of place. My head hung down looking for answers as I passed him by on my way inside.

My feet were dragging on the grass as I walked towards the open door of the house.

The suffering continued, but I was searching for hope and peace of mind. Playing on the swings was great joy and pain at Lynngate. The world was complicated for me at such a young age. Anyhow, Lynngate did not last forever.

Now, at that time, Bruce and Les were living with auntie, and in 1971 they went to live in Alberta Canada with their father.

CHAPTER 3

Life was worse after we moved to Yorkshire Road. My father lost the house at Tourmaline after he stopped paying the mortgage. There was a sense of failure around my parents. It was a very senseless and emotional time. They lost an awful lot of material things.

My heart was broken at the end, and my sister's attitude was changing for the worse. She was getting agitated with so much uncertainty in her life. Her friends were at Lynngate School.

My father was on his way to ruin. No one knew the truth about my father. However, our relatives knew our suffering.

At Yorkshire, I was 11 years old and a lot more social with the children in the neighbourhood. The baseball leagues at Yorkshire were well organized but I didn't participate. I was afraid to ask my father for money to join the league.

Anyway, I was there for my friends, but inside my heart I wanted to play.

My parents had no idea what they were doing to their lives. Yorkshire was hope. I saw my mother with a package in her hand as she walked off the bus with a smile on her face. In the package there was an automatic baseball game and it was great. I hugged and kissed my mother for the first time ever and that was a wonderful feeling. I will never forget the look on her face when we were laughing together. For the first time there was love in her heart. It hurt so much when I think back to that moment, but still the love I got from my mother was not all there. I said, "I love you mom," and laughing, she said nothing.

The baseball game was triumphant. It was a new day to try something different. I took the baseball game to London, England. The automatic baseball game was the greatest thing. That game was my Hall of Fame. I pretended to be like a real major leaguer and the New York Mets was the team to beat.

Denise and I took the bus to Lynngate School. My mind was way out in space as we travelled on the bus. Something strange was going on in the lives of our parents. Denise was a good sister. She kept me from falling apart at school. But I had to fight my own mental battles at home. My sister remembers the bad times and the frustrations of that time. I know her will and her determination, but her most important quality was her courage and the way she stood up for herself at that troubling time.

My sister had strong legs. She was an all-star catcher on her softball team. Her softball team was the champions of Scarborough. She was like Roy Campanella on the softball field.

In the summer of 1971, my father bought me a bicycle but there was no joy at all on my face or any feeling of love. I rode that bicycle that summer every day in a world without love.

Yorkshire was at times like Lynngate but for a shorter time. However, my father lost his job at the Ford Motor company. He became a troubled man after we left Yorkshire. My father would have been a millionaire at Tourmaline only if he had loved his family. At Tourmaline, he had it all and a beautiful house. My parents were at the top for a moment in time.

Now, we were going back to England to start over. My parents were a comedy of errors of great magnitude. They really didn't know what was best for their children. It was a mindless decision to move back to England. My sister and I would cross the Atlantic together for the last time. It was a terrible time for logical understanding. We were the children of the hopeless. A parachute was what I needed to prevent the tragedy that awaited me.

My sister and I were born in Hackney, London, England. Our mother put us on a boat to Antigua in 1962. My mother looked tired. Her mind would continuously wonder from time to time. She had too many foolish ideas about business. She would say, "England is a nice place."

Denise did not want to leave her best friend, Lynda Russell. They played softball together. I remember my sister's dynamic friend on the softball diamond. Lynda Russell was the greatest softball player that I had ever seen. She would hit a home run every time she came to the plate. She had the Jim Rice swing and the Darryl Strawberry hang time. Lynda would hit the ball a long way.

Anyhow, I didn't want to listen to any more of my mother's false hopes. Baseball was my only hope. There was no stability around my parents. The problems and confusion would not disappear from my parent's lives.

We left Yorkshire and I ended up living with Uncle Richard in his apartment before leaving for England. At the same time, my sister was staying with an aunt of ours, and my parents were with friends. We were all over the place. It was chaotic and shameful. It was a desperate time for my parents. There was no wisdom in their thoughts. My parents were on the run. Denise and I went from London to Antigua and from Antigua to Toronto and now back to London again.

My father travelled to England by himself. However, my mother never made it to England. Somehow she ended up in New York City. My mother was the blind leading the blind. My mother took advantage of her children. Real love was never around my parents. Denise and I were always in the way when we needed love.

Finally, we got on the airplane to London, England. It was a depressing flight for two children in a desperate situation. Denise was close to tears on the flight. We were growing up in a depressing situation and it was painful being exposed to such deep knife wounds. Later, I was thrown into a pit. We were the children of the lost and found. Reality was not a part of our lives. Nothing constructive was happening. I was in fear and so young and fragile in a world gone wrong.

The aircraft stopped somewhere in Scotland to refuel. The landscape around Scotland was beautiful. It was the perfect time for us to stretch our legs. I was trying to keep an open mind but my world was falling apart. It was hard to understand a world like this. My sister and I were on our own from the beginning, and I became confused with our new surroundings. Our Lives were on the ropes and that was reality.

CHAPTER 4

We landed at Heathrow airport and it was very busy. It was frightening to know what we left behind in Toronto. My father was standing there smiling beside a tall man. Both looked anxious and very happy to see us.

Mr. Charles was the man standing there with his son. He was my godfather and he called me "Moby Dick" after the great whale, "When you were a baby, you loved to eat that's why I gave you that name."

The winding roads of London were an exciting event with my godfather driving his car on what it looked like the wrong side of the road. We were on our way to the Charles home, where we would live for the time being. The house was small and joined together with the other houses on the street. Denise and I shared a bedroom together.

Mr. Charles was a very fashionable man, and his wife, Erin, was a great cook. She had a loveable personality.

Together, they had two children, Ian and Pat. The Charles family did their best to accommodate us in good faith, but my father was not helping them properly financially. He wanted to live for free.

London, England was too rainy and miserable looking, and the roads were narrow. The cars were all standard and small. The houses in the neighbourhood were old and without central heating. Gas stoves were used for cooking and kerosene was used in heaters to heat the homes in the winter. London was not in my heart; this was wrong from the beginning. England was ugly in the rain. There was no king Arthur and the round table.

Ian and I became friends. We played English football together, and I loved being the goalkeeper. Gordon Banks was my favourite footballer and the greatest goalkeeper according to the great Pele. Cricket and Football were the only games in town. Football was great for the children this was their passion to want to play for England.

Anyway, my sister was having a hard time adjusting. Tears were in her eyes when we first arrived at the Charles home. For some reason, she believed that I was mom's favourite, but Mrs. Charles said, "Your mother love both of you the same so stop that nonsense."

To tell the truth, my mother never existed in my mind when I got to England.

Denise became more irritable and mouthy with Mrs. Charles as time went on. They argued a few times in the house, and Mr. Charles had to be the peacemaker. My sister saw that her world was falling apart. When she started school, she began to settle down.

We went to Tottenham high school. North East London was like the movie To Sir with Love starring Sidney Poitier. The kids at school loved to fight and so did some of the teachers. It was wild at times in that poor neighbourhood.

I remember names like Tony Scott, Clifford Doby and Junior Edwards. Carl Barkley was the toughest kid in school and my best friend.

The young girls were bold and forward at school. I looked like one of the Jackson Five in 1972. But I was extremely shy, especially around girls, who seemed very aggressive. At Tottenham High School, my sister took good care of me. All we had was each other.

I was too young to know what was going on at the Charles home. My godfather had given up on my father. We were there long enough. And my father was not fooling anyone. It was time for him to get his life in order. At the end my Godfather was sad when saying goodbye to Denise and me.

After we left the Charles family, we went to live with old friends of my father's, Erie Willock and his family. His wife Bernita was a classy woman. Her household skills were impeccable. They had three children of their own.

It was the same old story with my father trying to con his friends, but he was running out of places to live. Mrs. Willock did not like him and it was obvious. She refused to tolerate his lies. Bernita treated my sister and I like her own. She was not into foolishness, and she made me feel very comfortable.

But it was a shame my father was up to no good again. He was a man without a conscience. Things got worse and the rumour was that he tried to sell the Willock house by pretending to be the owner. That was it; we were kicked out on the street with no place to go.

I was hurting deep down. It was a dark night and the streets were empty. My father and sister were setting the pace. I was walking behind my sister who was walking beside our father in the dark of the night. The long walk was disturbing. Only our footsteps were heard step by step. But where were we going? I kept on walking while looking at my feet for answers.

We had lost everything. Everything from Tourmaline Drive was gone, including my bubblegum cards, and the pain in my heart will never go away.

Finally, we came to the front of a filthy yard that had dead patches of grass and weed. The rusty gate was wide open, and beyond there was a huge house with wide glass windows. The night air was spring like when my father knocked on the front door. A young man with glasses answered the door. We came inside. Denise and I stood in the hallway while our father and the young man went into a room. I was standing there bewildered. My sister said to me, "This is an ugly house."

The conversation behind the door was getting louder and unclear. It was quite obvious that my father was in a desperate situation. I heard three voices in the room and one of the voices sounded unpleasant. The unpleasant voice was Uncle Stanley. After things settled down, Freestan, the young man, took Denise to his sister's home. No room was there for my sister.

I was living with three men in a room with one bed, and for the first time my sister and I were apart. It was hard and confusing the way we lived. The room was not an appropriate place to live with only one bed. Nothing at all was going right for me. My heart was crushed to pieces in that room. My life was not worth anything to that point.

Uncle Stanley was an alcoholic and a chain smoker. When drunk, he would provoke his wife who lived in another room right beside us. He would shout her name, "Albertine, Albertine, come out here." Freestan, his son, at times had to restrain him physically. Too much cursing was going on in that house.

The rooming-house had six other tenants. An African man was there with his wife, and Mac, a strange man, would give me pocket money. Everything was out of control. The bathroom was nasty and needed a new toilet. The kitchen was a mess and the basement abominable. I was afraid to go into the basement. I had to bathe at a public bath where I had to pay a fee. I was on my own.

London was wet and misty but not as cold as Toronto. The sun was hardly out in the wintertime, and Sinbad the dog was in the yard.

Many days I was in the house with nothing to eat. The cupboards were empty and nothing was in the refrigerator. I was starving in my uncle's house. Everyday I was so hungry. Sometimes Freestan would buy me fish and chips if I was lucky. However, many days, I would go to bed hungry. My stomach would growl and there were sores under my lip, and somehow I never went to school.

Freestan, my cousin, was perverted. He was the one who sexually assaulted me when I was a young boy. I had to perform oral sex or get beaten. I was sleeping in the same bed with an alcoholic and a pedophile. My father was on the couch in the same room. Freestan would physically assault me when no one was around. Somehow he was getting away with it. I couldn't go to my father. My father didn't care about me at all. It's hard to believe that no one knew what was going on. I was being abused in a crowded house with family members all around. I was crying out for help.

Freestan knew that my father didn't like me and that's why he took advantage of me. He knew that I was afraid of my father. My father knew what he was doing.

Night after night, Uncle Stanley was mostly preaching to me when he was drunk. "Your father is a liar and a thief, dear," that's what he said most of the time. His wife next door would scream out, "Stanley, stop preaching to that boy." "Albertine, shut up," he would say. Dealing with a drunk was difficult for a young boy like me.

I found a letter addressed to me hidden under a suitcase and it was opened. My uncle said, "Your father, that thief, opened that letter from your mother." The letter had money in it. Anyway, my uncle had a plan. He put the letter on the pillow where my father slept. Later that night, he came walking through the gate. Uncle Stanley and I pretended to be asleep by turning off the lights. When he turned on the lights he saw the letter on the pillow. He then made a mad dash for the suitcase and that's when my uncle opened his eyes and said, "What are you looking for? You opened the child's letter you damned thief." My father tried to deny it. Still I asked him for my money, and he slapped me in the face angrily. From the couch, he told my uncle that he preferred my sister. Uncle Stanley was right. In the first place, he didn't want my father under his roof. Uncle Stanley was straightforward and honest. He drank ginger wine like water and smoked a lot of senior service cigarettes.

My situation was getting worse. I was suffering from malnutrition. London was a desperate time for me in 1972. Many times I would cry out for help but no one came. Freestan was physically and sexually abusing me in the day and there had to be someone there at least once. My uncle cared to some extent but he had his own problems with alcoholism. He was kind-hearted and a drunk at the same time.

Again, I was an innocent boy living with an alcoholic and a child molester, that's the way it was. I was in a different world. I had no time to worry about my sister. Relatives came but nothing was done about my hunger. Nonsense was all around me.

Many times I would think back to Lynngate to remember my bubblegum cards. My stomach would growl in the daytime. There was nothing to eat. The radio was my only solace. Songs by Slade and T Rex kept me from going insane. They played Get Back Honky Cat by Elton John every day along with the Jackson Five and Rod Stewart's You Wear It Well. K.C. Jones was on the television in the morning and then it was the sport of Cricket in the afternoon.

No compassion was in my father's heart. I was starving and there was nothing to do but lie on the bed. The radio drowned some of my sorrows.

Uncle Stanley had many children, but none of them did much for the starving boy. They came and saw nothing. His daughter Carolie was looking after Denise. Carolie was very responsible. "The boy says he is starving," she would say to my father. She knew who my father was and she told me the truth. Carolie had a pit-bull personality. Miss Cochrane was a lot like Carolie.

My father was a gambler. He would rather spend his money on dogs and horses, and he was getting away with not feeding me. He was destroying his own life and at the same time trying to destroy me.

You can't imagine how hungry I was at times. At one time I couldn't eat, and a few times Keith would take me to his home for dinner. Keith was Uncle Stanley's son. I was skin and bones at the time. I was starving in front of my family. However, Keith tried to show some compassion, but he was far away from my heart.

It was getting more difficult to communicate, and there were times when I thought I was going to die from hunger and from the shame and humiliation of sexual abuse. My family stood there and watched me suffer. I could do nothing.

My body was frail and weak. My family had disappeared. I heard footsteps in the hallway when I was being abused, but no one seemed to hear me crying. Life was hell in London without my mother. The tenants were not in the right position to help. They knew that someone in my family was wicked. It was over.

Finally, the authorities took me away from my father. I remember the young woman in her blue uniform and how she was staring at me. I was at the police station, and my eyes were glued to the floor. She said to me, "Please, I would like you to take off your clothes." I was a scared young boy. Emotionally, I felt tortured by the outside world. No one that I knew cared about me, but somehow I was in good hands for the first time since I left Johnson's Point. My mind was on a lot of things at that moment, but that moment with that woman was frightening. As I stood there in my underwear, the look of astonishment was on her face. She was looking at a boy suffering from malnutrition. It was frightening the way my ribs were sticking out. I was weak and in a lot of pain. She asked me questions but I said nothing. She knew that there was something wrong. She was the lady with many concerns. Her young face looked horrified. I don't know how the authorities found out about me. I don't even remember being removed from my uncle's house. All I know was that one day I found myself in a police station.

The same day I met Mr. Dean who was a social worker. He was a tall East Indian man who showed genuine concern for my welfare. He was good to me. He tried his best to make sure that I was in a better situation. Child Services were there when I was in rough shape. Mr. Dean carried himself like a true gentleman. It was a long time ago when he made me a cup of tea. I remember him saying, "You must be hungry." His eyes squinted in disbelief while looking at my emaciated physique.

Mr. Dean drove me to a group home for unwanted children. It was a very lonely drive. He said, "I want you to call me to let me know that you are okay." He was concerned about me to the very end.

The children were staring at me in the doorway. I had nothing but the clothes on my back. The first day at the group home will remain in my heart forever. I was living in a home with other unfortunate children. It was hard for me to make eye contact. I was scared at first, and it took me a while to make the adjustment. It was a pleasant place to be in with lots of food to eat.

However, an older boy named Brian tried to bully me. He would yell, "Who are you looking at?" at the breakfast table. At that time, the children would call me names like Biafra. Biafra was a ravaged African nation. Some of the young children of Biafra had huge stomachs and were suffering from malnutrition.

James Bunting stood up for me when things got out of hand. I watched him slap Brian in the face. Brian was afraid of James and I saw it in his eyes. He didn't want to fight James. After that episode with James, Brian and I became more comfortable. I survived the group home with James' help. He was the Good Samaritan. It was an incredible feeling to know that James was going to fight for me. With time, Brian became a better person.

The group home gave me the chance to get healthy. I was happier being apart from my father. But to my surprise, Freestan came to visit me. He knew where I was. He was a troubled man. My father visited also. Both were despicable and pathetic. They were responsible for that tragic time. Even though he made an appearance, my father's heart was not there. He never wanted the responsibility.

Many days I would think back to my days at Tourmaline Drive when I had bubblegum cards in my pockets. I remember being hungry on the bed lying down while listening to the radio. The dog in the yard had food to eat. Before I came to the group home, my heart was full of hurt. I needed to get away from my father who was trying to destroy my life. At the same time, I didn't know how to express myself to others. I was severely neglected by my own people. I was twelve years old and on my own. Fear and uncertainty was in my world.

I was taken to the dentist by Tony, a staff member. One tooth was so bad that the doctor wanted to put me to sleep to remove it. Immediately I started to cry and I needed a lot of reassurance after shouting, "I am not going to wake up. I don't want to be put to sleep." I was afraid of the unconscious. Tony had to calm me down. Anyway, I was put to sleep. When I woke up, I started crying again although Tony was there to hold my hand.

I found laughter at the time when I was suffering. The group home was a peaceful environment. It was fun and the food was good. Being isolated from my family was the greatest thing, but it didn't last.

Somehow I was back living with my father and there was more pain and heartache to follow. It was the same old thing. We stayed here and there with his friends. Still no one questioned what my father was doing to my life. At times, I didn't know if I was going to survive in my surroundings. It was hell. I was in the wrong hands.

I remember the Christmas when my father sent me to the Willock's home for dinner, but he made no prior arrangements with them. I was going there every evening to eat. My father was wicked at that time. He knew what he was doing. Bernita had to tell me the truth and it was humiliating. She tried not to hurt my feelings and I respected her. My father's reaction was strange when I questioned him about what Bernita said to me about him. He said, "You think I send you there to beg food?" My father was a liar and a thief. That's exactly what Uncle Stanley said to me in the room of horrors. It was a painful episode.

A cousin of mine told me, "Wait until you're eighteen." The pressure was on while I searched for my way out of hell.

My will to survive was in great jeopardy. I became a troubled young boy, and I was becoming very temperamental.

At that time, I was living with my cousin Mister Green. He was good to me from the beginning. He knew how to talk to me but he was not father-like. My cousin never mentioned my father. They were like night and day.

Later on, my father said to me that he was going back to Toronto and I was to stay with Mr. Green until later when he would send for me. I told him that I would stay put. My father was out of bounds. A fool I was not. He never wanted me from the beginning. He was packing his clothes before disappearing into the dark of the night.

That night when Mr. Green came home, he asked me for my father. I told him that he went to Toronto. My cousin was shocked when I told him that he was to look after me. He said, "What? Your father never told me that he was going to Toronto. Are you sure? He never told me anything like that." My father abandoned me on the streets of London and that became a very desperate situation. Mr. Green was not in any position to look after me and his attitude began to change. I felt unwanted. No accommodation was made for me.

Mr. Green took me to see Uncle Malcolm, my mother's brother by father. They had no idea what to do with me. No one wanted the responsibility. Malcolm was somewhat vague when asking me, "Did your daddy say why he left you?" The concern for me was very poor. No one wanted to take me in. A stranger said, "Why would Claxton leave his son behind?" It was unbelievable. On the street I was again looking for a place to sleep. The year 1972 was a catastrophe without my mother. Family love was far from me.

At the same time, I learned that my sister was back in Toronto. Again, nothing was making sense. The world was swallowing me up and my childhood was becoming a tragedy. My relatives were too lackadaisical when showing concern about my welfare. They did nothing to help me in London. My heart was crying out for help. I was standing on the streets of London in a lot of pain. I was helpless at that moment in time. By now my father was back in Toronto and they were all there to greet him at the airport. They were surprised to see him without me.

Somehow, I was back with Child Services, and Mr. Dean looked distraught and wanted to know why I didn't call him. "What happened? Why didn't you call me?" he asked. He looked worried. He was sincere and he came a long way to see me. I was out of his district and out of his hands, that's why he was so frustrated. It was a troubling time mentally. Mr. Dean wanted the responsibility even though he didn't have the authority. He had a grim look on his face, which was real and genuine. This time, Social Services put me in a different group home, which was more sophisticated than the first one. This new home was a family-style setting. The children were taught how to eat properly with a knife and fork around the table, and the bedrooms were very nice with wall-to-wall carpeting.

I was alone with my thoughts and feelings. It was difficult to participate with the other children. My emotions were deep inside of my heart. No one came to see me and that was great. I had to be content with myself.

The Jackson Five was on the radio and I would sing and dance to their songs. Got To Be There was the song that was most popular in 1972.

However, my education was suffering. I attended two other schools after leaving Tottenham High. I can remember how isolated I felt every time I started a new school. Everyone would stare at me. It was difficult to learn in my situation.

Immediately I said, "I don't want to go," when a staff member at the group home said to me that my father was sending an airplane ticket for me for a flight to Toronto. She said, "We can't do anything about this. He is your father." This was the first time that I displayed any type of hateful emotion directed towards my father. I wanted nothing to do with the plane ticket that was coming. That very night I couldn't sleep and there were many horrible thoughts in my head. What was going to happen next? It was 1973. I was almost a teenager and I was angry with my world. My flight to Toronto was long and agonizing.

CHAPTER 5

My trip to London, England was over, but the pain will last a lifetime. I saw my father standing there at the airport. He was the bad guy. Right away I said, "Where is Denise?" I despised him. I said, "I don't want to go with you. Where is mom?" but he said nothing. He knew that I hated him. Angrily he said, "Just come ahead boy." I had no idea where we were going. On the bus, I sat far away from him.

I walked up the stairs, and the door to the small house was open. Denise was inside cooking. She looked puzzled when she saw me standing in the kitchen. She gave me the unbelievable look. She said, "What's going on? Mom is on her way to England to look for you." Our father was pretending that he didn't know.

It was a pathetic situation for my mother and me. My mother and I were travelling at the same time. When I was landing in Toronto, she was landing in London. It was a great manoeuvre and my father's doing. He didn't want my mother and me together. He was hiding something.

Nevertheless, my mother stayed in England for three years and that was a foolish thing for her to do. She lived with Uncle Stanley in the same room where I was abused.

Denise was 14 and she was becoming hotheaded. Her father was trying to ruin her life.

We lived at 606 Ossington Avenue in a rooming house. We had to share the bathroom with other tenants. Ossington Avenue at that time was full of a lot of European emigrants. A Greek family owned the house where we stayed. The owner didn't like my father. My father was too inconsistent when paying bills. He was like that all the time. The neighbourhood was good with good people. Toronto was good in the early 70's.

The very same day, I rushed to the store to buy a pack of baseball cards and an ice-cream sandwich. I wanted things to be like it was at Lynngate School.

Dewson Street Junior Public School was fun. There were a lot of outdoor activities to keep me busy. I remember the girl who had a crush on me, but I was too shy talking to her and her friend. I was practically running away from relationships. Anyway, my heart went into exile after London.

A lot of time was spent sitting on my bed with my baseball cards. It was in the library where I started reading a lot of baseball books. That's where my mind was most of the time. Being obsessed with a particular baseball book, that's the way I was. Baseball statistics fascinated me. The pictures of the great baseball players of the past were magnificent. Loneliness inspired me to read about the Babe and the Brooklyn Dodgers. The great Negro Leagues were an education and I believed that I was a part of them. It was like I knew them from a long time ago. The star of baseball was my homework. Nothing was more important. I was a teenager now in 1973, the year the Mets won the pennant. I knew more about baseball than anyone else.

There were problems with my behaviour at Kent Senior High School. My concentration was not there. I was doing poorly. Kent was a tough school academically and I was falling behind, and it was hard for me to understand the laughter of my classmates. My world was not the same as theirs. Participating in class was difficult. Most times, my mind was elsewhere. The kids were getting too close and my attitude was getting me in trouble. I didn't like my surroundings. I was not into friends. There were times when I wanted to scream at the foolishness at public school. It was hard to disappear in a crowded world of many problems. They wanted to know me but I definitely did not want to know them.

My feelings were hurt deeply after I received 86% on a botany exam, which was the second highest mark in the class. I bragged loudly and boasted about it. The teacher told the class, "If you don't keep quiet I am going to take 20% off your mark." There was an announcement on the public address system. He caught me talking so he reduced my mark to 66%.

My classmates were laughing at me. I became angry with the science teacher and a classmate came into my face laughing and was being malicious. I started punching him many times between the door and the hallway, bloodying his nose. Passing by, the French teacher stopped me. She took me to the vice principal's office where I spent a few days. There was no reason to apologize for something like that, that's the way I thought. The vice principal gave me lectures about my behaviour but my mind was elsewhere. I refused to listen to him. Later that day, the science teacher came by to see if I was still upset. I was, certainly, so then he restored my mark back to 86% and I was glad.

Regardless, school was not a great idea for me in 1973. Anger was created in me from my stay in England. It was complicated and sour. I had no parental guidance. I became frustrated for not being able to communicate with the world even though the world knew that I was in trouble. Nevertheless, I had to move on. Still, I was looking for that father figure.

That summer, I started working for Dickey Dee Ice Cream. I made a few dollars while on the sidewalks. To my surprise, I met Mr. Charles again when I was selling ice cream. He was happy to see me. He told me that he came to Toronto to visit relatives. My godfather was a polished man. He never mentioned my father's name.

Most of my money was spent on bubblegum cards and my sister. It was good to see her smile again.

Sometime that summer in 1973, my father was in jail. Denise and I went to the police station to pick up the rent money. He was in handcuffs when he came out to meet us.

Again, we were on the move. I vaguely remember the neighbourhood where we were living, and I changed schools again. Ledbury Park Public School was the new school.

Baseball was my escape. The New York Mets beat the mighty big red machine with the great Tom Seaver and Jerry Koosman. Rusty Staub was the star of the show. However, the Oakland A's won the World Series with Mr. October, Reggie Jackson. At the same time, I was being battered and bruised mentally from the outside.

I was getting older. The presence of my father was the problem. I was trying to find my way without him, but he made things impossible. Our suitcases were always packed wherever we were. Wisdom was nowhere to be found. My father was a constant nuisance. He was not a good person. He was without love. My father was always lying down on the couch watching television like a lazy cartoon character.

He seldom went to work while complaining about his back many times. He was a part of this mean world. Anyhow, I had my bubblegum cards and my baseball books to read that was important in my world.

Now my sister and I began spending our weekends with Uncle Richard. He was my father's younger brother and that was hard to believe. He was the complete opposite of his brother. Uncle Richard was family-first. He took his responsibilities seriously. There was always a place to sleep and food to eat at his home. He had three young children and a very sincere and generous wife. Elaine, my uncle's wife, treated Denise and I like gold. They made room for us even though they didn't have much.

Uncle Richard and I watched baseball together while talking about family and black history. His feelings were honest. He made some sacrifices for us at the expense of his own children. My sister and Uncle Richard were the best of friends. I would listen to music and watch baseball for survival. It was so depressing going back home to wherever we lived. There was a sad feeling of disappointment when the weekend was over.

We were on the move again. My sister was angry with our father. They argued a lot but nothing was solved. I did witness them having a fistfight. My sister had enough, but still the nonsense continued. I wouldn't have survived my father without God.

There was a time when Denise and I went to live with my mother's sister, Aunt Doris. She lived at Jane and Sheppard. Her home was like a sanctuary and my bedroom was very much like Lynngate. She was married with a young child.

My mother and aunt did not get along. She was more educated than my mother, but something was always on my aunt's mind. She was trapped in her moody silence and was very particular in her ways. Her home was polished with a complex design. My aunt liked things organized. She wanted things to be done without question. However, her home was my home, and she was too uptight at times with her husband.

He played reggae music in the basement. It was great music, that's the music I adore. He was a pleasant man who stayed by himself. He never interfered with Denise and me. His daughter loved him.

My aunt and I were friends, but my sister and she were always at odds. It was hard to understand my aunt at times. It was tough to make her laugh. Anyhow, she wanted the best for us. It was the first time in a long while that we were cared for properly.

Again, I started another public school. Beverly Heights was the fourth school I attended within a year and a half. It was hard to stay focused and make lasting friendships when I was an adolescent. I went to seven schools within two years beginning with Tottenham.

I remember starting a fight with a classmate who was acting macho. He thought I was afraid of him. My attitude came from the group home in London. I was not a fighter or a troublemaker. However, I disliked anyone who was too mouthy. I had few friends but I was known for being emotional. It was time for me to try and save myself from destruction.

At that time, we were all doing the Robot Dance to the Michael Jackson song, Dancing Machine. Watergate was the political discussion, and Hank Aaron broke the Babe's home—run record. Also, that was the time when I met Charlie Craib and his family.

Looking through the windows, I saw a young boy with a hockey stick playing alone. I finally went over to where he was and asked him for a game. He said, "I don't care." We played there and everywhere for years. Charlie was the best of times. We were from two different worlds. Our friendship was everlasting. It was a miracle from the beginning. We never fought or argued. We competed with and against each other for years. Our friendship was cordial and full of life.

Charlie brought me to his home. His brother was my brother and his sisters were my sisters, and his mother became my mother and his father was my father. This family was love. It was the right time to move forward. It was where I wanted to be. Charlie's family knew how to show love.

They had a different temperament. I became a part of them and goodness came to my heart.

Charlie and I played wall ball, a simulated baseball game in the summer at the schoolyard that resembled Fenway Park. I found joy for a short time. Wall ball was real baseball, pitcher verses hitter. We pretended to be like real major leaguers. Charlie was a good pitcher. There were times when I couldn't hit his pitches. I was more of a thrower with a powerful arm and a hitter with power, but we were even when it came to wins and losses.

My time with Charlie reminded me of Lynngate with my bubblegum cards. He was a spoiled boy who quit school at 16, but he was more intelligent than most. The summers with Charlie were long and sweet.

Mrs. Craib was love and the mother I always wanted. She knew how to love. Her children were full of love and kindness. There were real feelings of love which I received from that family. Mrs. Craib took care of her children and gave them lectures and I would listen. Her generosity and sincerity were real. I understood love in a real family for the first time in 1974. They were living in a home full of love and I was always there. The Craibs were like the Brady Bunch. They were not pretenders. Their love was unconditional.

The summer of 74 was quite interesting when Bruce and Les came to Toronto. They were older. Johnson's Point was over. Nothing was there emotionally anymore. Miss

Cochrane came to visit also. It was a Johnson's Point reunion. We were not babies anymore. We didn't know each other. However, Miss Cochrane and I remained close forever, but the significance of that time was gone.

At the same time, my aunt's house was full of many relatives. Still my parents were unaccounted for. I was getting a lot of headaches being under a lot of stress from my past. The comic book heroes from that time were Iron Fist and the Master of Kung Fu. Bruce loved comic books. Les was more athletic and outgoing.

Bruce was more into himself somewhat. He was not a sportsman. There were some intense arguments and fighting between Bruce and Les that summer. The summer to remember was coming to an end.

The problem now was the way I was being educated. In Johnson's Point the schools were more disciplined. There were inspections every day. Our hands and fingernails had to be clean. They encouraged us to read out loud and it was important to learn how to spell. Also, we prayed every day for the soul and it was good. On Fridays, the children had to clean the schoolyard, which was another form of discipline.

Canadian schools were poor. The teachers gave too many lectures. We did not have to memorize any nursery rhymes. The teachers were programmed and that was dull. They were collecting a fat paycheck from their pension. The teachers were not that helpful. I needed help in areas like the liberal arts.

Some children in London had no manners. The classroom was in chaos with some of the teachers. I was suffering a lot in school. At Tottenham, the children would bang their desks to distract the teachers from teaching. The teachers were part of the problem. The children wore uniforms to look smart and the ones on report were in trouble. The education system was out of order in London. Some of the teachers were not dedicated enough to teach.

In my situation, it was baseball that motivated me, that was my way. Junior high was baseball and girls, that's how it was for me in the early seventies. I graduated from Beverly Heights Junior High School, which was my one and only graduation.

CHAPTER 6

C.W. Jeffery's on Sentinel Road was the high school I went to in 1975. It was a fashion school and I was there for three years, but I didn't graduate. My sister started there before me in 1974.

On my first day, I almost got into a fight with a senior on the stairs. I was going into grade 10 with other things on my mind. C.W. Jeffery's High School at that time had the most beautiful girls in North York.

I was depressed at high school from nine o'clock until three o'clock. Listening to constant dictation every day was torture while moving from class to class. There was nothing there for me. I would bring my baseball magazines to school to keep my head from exploding. It was so dull that I had to talk hockey all winter. The Montreal Canadians hockey team was awesome in the 70's and the team to beat.

The majority of my classmates at C.W. Jeffery's were Italians and they were good people. I loved their enthusiasm and sense of humour. My Italian friends took very good care of me.

Angela Tortolo was the most beautiful Italian girl in grade 10 and she had a crush on me, but I didn't know how to handle that with so many scars on my heart. It was not puppy love. She will always remain in my heart.

At times high school was unbearable, especially with me watching the clock. My classmates gave me a lot of space. I was a time-bomb ticking. I was the one who stood up to Bernard Trainer, the bully. I threw punches to help the weak, and I had two awesome fights inside the classroom. The teachers had no idea what to do with me.

Anyway, my Liberal education was poor. Sure, C.W. Jeffery's was an academic school. The curriculum had Italian, Latin and Roman History.

However, there was no black history in the curriculum. Where were the black heroes? My liberal education was oppression.

Mr. Faraday, my grade 10 history teacher, made me and my classmates watch a film that depicted blacks as being lazy. Mr. Faraday was working on black children's self-esteem. I knew then that Canadian high schools were oppressive. Mr. Faraday was not Italian.

All children should be taught black history in North America. Canadian history was taught without the acknowledgement of black people, which was a shameful exercise. Ethiopia was black history which was part of the Garden of Eden and that's important history for all children. My teachers were not educated properly in history.

Anyhow, I took notes in class and tried to make sense out of nonsense. For example, Louis Riel was not a traitor. He was fighting for the freedom of his people, the Metis. The Canadian Government had no right to hang an innocent man charged with treason.

My classmates were growing up without the knowledge of the truth. They were at their lockers talking about homework but I wasn't interested. High school was taking too long. I wanted the three years to go by quickly. My mind was deep inside of my soul, and it was dark, that side of my consciousness. Miss Cochrane never nurtured me to be subservient to the world around me that's why I questioned everything in my high school.

Black children are not given the proper liberal arts education and that's why it's so difficult for them to survive in North America. For myself, I went to the library to find my history and to find the truth. I do remember when I was asked why I wanted to know so much about the Negro Leagues. The Negro Leagues taught me about Jim Crow and oppression. I knew that the Declaration of Independence was not written for the Negro Leagues when I was in High School. The Declaration of Independence was Jim Crow. The library was where I found my freedom in an oppressive institution, which was C.W. Jeffery's.

Baseball did rejuvenate me at times when my mind was constantly thinking on the run. My mind would wonder continuously. My dreams were dreams. There was no hope for the future with no father to stand beside me. I was swimming the Atlantic without a life jacket. The pain was getting worse even though I was a popular guy in high school by the time I was in grade eleven.

I played football for one year and it was good. I was a defensive back and a starter. I mastered that position. The football coach was one of the very few teachers who communicated well with black children. Mr. Bobby Pierce was the football coach and a good human being. He gave me a lot of confidence and he made me a starter on the kickoff team. He was a special guy and a good football coach.

I enjoyed Egyptian history. The ancient Egyptians were black. Miss Little, my teacher, congratulated me for writing the best paper on ancient Egypt.

In my last year at Jeffery's, I met Joanne Walker from Barbados. She was beautiful and my first true love. I loved her although she was in grade ten. Many times I was not a good boyfriend in our relationship. We were to marry and ride off on a white horse to paradise. She pampered me but I was distant. Our relationship did not last. She found someone else.

Again, my sister and I were living with our father for a short time. He was living with another woman at that time. I had to go to another house to sleep in the evenings; there was no room for me again. But I still went to C.W. Jeffery's High School.

The confusion continued. Back and forth, Denise and I went back to live with Aunt Doris, and sometime before grade eleven our mother came back from London, England. The three of us were living together for the first time since Yorkshire. My mother and father were now divorced but it was too late.

Aunt Doris could not live with my mother. They had philosophical differences. My mother wanted someone to look after her children while she hops around the world. There was nothing pure in my mother's heart. She loved people's company while trying to give them the impression that she was a good mother. I didn't like my mother from the beginning. She didn't know how to love at all.

We moved across the street to 2600 Jane Street. I believe that my aunt had had enough of her sister. I wanted to be free from my mother. She would talk a lot of nonsense about my father, something was wrong with her thinking. She was always talking to herself and that was very troubling.

CHAPTER 7

I was 18 and high school was almost over. The summer of 1978 was when I ended up in summer school. Before that I did register for college and that was the time when I began to change.

That summer I started smoking cigarettes and marijuana at summer school. Spider and Desi from summer school bought the drugs. When they had it I smoked it, which was something to do. I wasn't hooked on drugs at all. I never smoked at home. I drank slowly and I was out late at nights hanging around the town with Spider. Spider wore his heart on his sleeve. For me he was a highlight with a great sense of humour. Spider was good to me. At one time, he carried a gun for his protection.

For me baseball was the most important adventure. Mentally I wasn't into doing anything. Charlie and I rarely played wall ball anymore. I was straying away from the ballpark. Too often I was hanging out in the wrong places. But Spider was there at all times when I needed someone to talk to. I was his best friend.

That fall I was studying chemistry by correspondence; I needed two more credits to graduate from high school. I got accepted for college with the understanding that I would finish high school but I never did. The fall of 1978 was when the New York Yankees broke the hearts of Red Sox fans with the Bucky Dent home run that sailed over the green monster. Reggie Jackson won the World Series for the Yankees in the late 70's.

As time went on, I found out that Humber College was not for me. I was unable to get my head into the books. My friend Jungles and I hung out in the concourse with the nurses and the fashion designers. My student loan was spent at the disco and on new clothes but I was very depressed. I was making friends with a lot of the ladies at College.

Still my childhood was haunting me. There was no dedication to my studies at all. It was tough mentally to be around my mother. My loan was spent in the nightclubs and I was there two times a week. Downtown, I was hanging out with the pimps and hookers while dancing the night away.

My mother was getting angry at me for coming home late at nights. She talked about her brother, Kelso Cochrane, who was stabbed to death by Teddy Boys in Notting dale late at night in south London. Kelso had his hand in a sling when he was stabbed to death by six white youths.

There were times when I wanted to punch my mother in the face. Her head was like stone. My mother was child like with her head full with a lot of nonsense. My sister would scream at her to leave me alone.

Anyway, I had my baseball cards and books to read, and I played my simulated baseball board games to keep me from going insane at home. I stopped playing wall ball for no reason. Charlie and I were on different paths but he will always be my greatest childhood friend. He never came to where I lived and that was no coincidence.

I was still staying out late on school nights. Right across the street from home, I would eat alone in the restaurant. I was also smoking a lot and drinking in the nightclubs. Then later I would pass out on the bed with my clothes on with the room light shining on my face. While waking up with the light on, I didn't know what was going on in my head.

It was a difficult time. I couldn't make it to college in the mornings. I became addicted to cigarettes and I was lightheaded. Spider would throw cold water in my face when I got too high. When thinking about my life as a teenager, I would get so depressed. My fingers would shake from nervousness. I was hiding from a horrible experience.

There was a night when I gave a stranger my expensive gold ring in a nightclub, but somehow on my way back home I didn't know that it was missing from my finger. I thought I had left the ring in my bedroom. It took me awhile to remember that I gave the ring to a stranger.

At times, my mind was far away from reality. I remember pulling my sister's legs while she was sitting. I was laughing with her while high in the sky.

I was failing college even though I changed programs halfway through. I was studying electronics. It was difficult to stay awake in college. Something was wrong.

Again, my mother was gone. I believe she went to New York to visit her half-sister by father. My mother was a desperate woman.

CHAPTER 8

I was walking home north on Jane Street across Sheppard Avenue. It was springtime in 1979. My world was about to fall apart again, and emotionally I was not ready to confront my childhood.

We lived at 2600 Jane Street on the 11th floor of an apartment building right across from the pool hall. I opened the door and found my sister sewing her clothes. My sister was too confrontational at times. "Hi Gladstone," she said when I came through the door.

My body felt wiry as I dropped down on the couch. Immediately, I stood up and said to my sister, "Denise, something is going to happen to me." Right away something strange blew upon me, then a twitch in my chest. Then right away my heart started to pound and there was great pain. It was unbelievable. I started screaming, "I am having a heart attack" while rubbing my chest. My heart was making an unusual sound. Denise started screaming, "What's wrong, what's wrong?" I opened the door and ran down the hallway of the building screaming. "I am having a heart attack." I thought I was going to die. I ran down the hallway screaming while rubbing my chest in a circular motion. I pushed the elevator buttons before running back into the apartment.

My sister passed the telephone to me and said, "Auntie is on the phone." My aunt asked me, "Did you have anything to eat today, drink some water?" I was calm for a moment but the pain came back and my heart started to pound. I dropped the phone and ran out of the apartment and down the steps from the 11ᵗʰ floor and into a variety store screaming, "I am having a heart attack call an ambulance." I was rubbing my chest while pacing back and forth.

Everyone in the store gave me that look of astonishment. The clerk had no idea what to say or do. I ran out of the store and into the parking lot. That's when I saw a cab and I stopped it frantically and saying hurry to the cab driver, "I am having a heart attack, take me to the hospital." The cab driver said, "Come in, come in, don't worry." The cab driver was a black man and he was concerned as we talked on the way to the hospital. It was a frightening experience. As soon as I got to the hospital, I quickly left the cab without paying. Anyway, the cab driver never came into the hospital for his fee. The cab driver was in the right place that night when I thought I was going to die.

I was in great panic in emergency at York Finch Hospital. The woman sitting at the counter was taking her time asking questions like, "What's your family doctor's name?" There was no urgency in her voice. "Please, lady, my heart is killing me." "Just relax, sir, the doctor will see you now."

The doctor mentioned that it might be a mild cardiac arrest. He also wanted to know if I was a drug user. "The tests showed, sir, that you have a virus in the urine." The nurse did a cardiogram to check my heart, which was fine. Finally, the doctor gave me a prescription for water pills to flush out my system and recommended that I see my family doctor.

My aunt was at the hospital and she was getting agitated. "How long is this going to take? I have to go to work in the morning," talking to herself. It was a long stay at the hospital. My mother was in New York at this time.

My aunt was talking to me about my medication and seeing the family doctor. All night long I was lying down on my stomach while listening to my heart pound. Pain was still there.

In the morning I went to see Doctor Mandel for a complete check-up and x-rays. The stomach x-rays showed that I had ulcers. I was taking water pills for the virus in the urine and Stelabid for the ulcers. I became paranoid when taking my medication. I was watching the clock to make sure that I was taking the pills on time. Everything I did was on schedule. My health was on my mind constantly. If I felt uncomfortable I would rush back to the doctor for reassurance. Doctor Mandel would repeat the same tests over and over again. I had chest x-rays, brain scans and cardiograms with the same results being normal.

My college education was coming to an end. It was difficult to focus with my heart on my mind. Before I left Humber College for good, I talked to my friend Jungles about my condition. He saw my hand shaking. Jungles told me his sister died a year earlier from a brain hemorrhage.

Doctor Mandel was not convincing enough, "Mr. Matthew, your chart shows that your heart is normal." But still I felt uncomfortable and I wanted a second opinion. I called my best friend, Charlie, and I said to him, "Charlie, can you come with me to the doctor?" Charlie said, "Sure, what time?" I said, "for 11 o'clock, okay?" On the bus, my heart started acting up again so I got up and walked around. Charlie was trustworthy; he never said anything about my illness.

Doctor Sara was my father's physician. He looked at me and said, "You're very tall. Don't worry, your heart is strong." However, Doctor Sara gave me another prescription, which was a milder sedative for my ulcers. I became frustrated with the whole situation so I went back to Doctor Mandel. He said, "Your chart shows that you have ulcers and you have to stick to one doctor." He was trying to be as honest as possible.

It was a nightmare and my mind was constantly on my heart. My mother was not supportive. She made me feel like I was pretending, "Come on," she would say, "Get on with it." She was insensitive. My mother behaved like a child at times.

I was breaking down emotionally in front of Doctor Mandel. I started crying saying, "I don't like my mother." Doctor Mandel said, "I think you're having a nervous breakdown." He was writing on a piece of paper before he called a cab to take me to the hospital.

The secretary standing there in the hospital was very attractive. She gave me a cup of water to drink. Then along came a man who took the letter from the secretary and said, "I am going to admit you." He was Doctor Cooper, the psychiatrist.

My fragile childhood was stuck in my heart. It was time to tell the truth about my past.

I was admitted to the Psychiatric Ward at York Finch Hospital in May of 1979, the same year the Pittsburgh Pirates won the World Series with the great Willie Stargel.

I was worried about having a heart attack, but that was all in my mind according to my chart, and the dark places in my heart were coming out.

I was pacing the floor and rubbing my chest, and I was angry at the way my life was. My mother didn't know how to love. Sometimes I would catch her talking to herself continuously. She would say ugly things like, "You're just like your father." My mother was not interested in my feelings. My father was mean to me when I was a child.

On the ward, I was anxious most of the time. Doctor Cooper said that I was in an acute anxiety state. He prescribed Valium, a psychiatric drug. Psychiatric medication was tough on my body physically. My mouth was dry and I was thirsty a lot of times. The medication created bizarre side-effects.

Doctor Mandel visited me almost every day. He had a great bedside manner. The ward was very clean, and I shared a bedroom with another patient for a short time. I believe that my heart was the problem even though the charts say something different.

Doctor Cooper was a pompous man. He was not interested in what I had to say. He would repeat, "Gladstone, you're fine." He was head of Psychiatry at York Finch and he showed a lot of arrogance. I was a black man in the Canadian mental health system, which was a nightmare.

After breakfast, it was medication time and then back to the living room to sit and wait for the doctor. The living room had a table and comfortable chairs to sit on at meal times, and there was a television and magazines to read.

The other patients were drugged and that affected their movements, which was slow. I noticed that some of the patients had unusual mood swings. Psychiatric medication in 1979 made things worse for the severely depressed, and the nurses were there to enforce the taking of drugs.

The pain around my heart would not go away. My heart was racing and it was difficult to cope. The psychiatric ward at York Finch hospital was not good. I thought the nurses were too full of themselves. I tried to explain my situation with my mother to them but it didn't matter. I was sitting there worried about my heart and the problems that concern my family. The pain does not go away.

Relaxation therapy and bed-rest were very important. The hospital food was good and in small portions. My girlfriend, Tina, from Sweden visited me and so did my father. My father said, "I am the one responsible for you being here." That was the first time that I heard compassion in my father's voice. He sure sounded genuine. My mother said that I was running away from my responsibilities. She was who she was.

Charlie came to the hospital to visit and he gave me a baseball book called the Pride of the Yankees, the story of the great Yankees hero, the iron horse, Lou Gehrig. Gehrig said, "I am the luckiest man on the face of the earth." And he was dying. His story was my inspiration.

The nurses wanted only to talk about my acute anxiety state and my psychological problem according to my chart. The drugs were causing me to fall asleep in the middle of the day. Anyway, my heart was back to normal, I believe, and there was a big smile on Doctor Cooper's face. It was time for a discharge.

I went to live with my aunt at Jane and Finch. I wanted nothing to do with my mother. Everything in my life was falling apart. Jane and Finch was a beautiful place in 1979. At that time, my aunt was getting a divorce and living with her daughter in a beautiful condominium.

I was slow and weary at a very frustrating time. Psychiatric drugs were beginning to take over my body. My mother wanted me to think that I had a mental illness. She was trying to get rid of me.

I began thinking about my troubled past, and I became paranoid with my mind in space. There was anxiousness and desperation in my life. My family had abandoned me. My heart was acting up again one night. I couldn't sleep and my legs were getting hot while lying down in bed with my heart racing. It was a frightening feeling listening to my heart pound. The pain would not leave my consciousness.

I told my aunt that I was going to die. She started to cry at the same time saying, "Go back to your mother, I can't take it anymore." My mother was never there for me. So I went back to the hospital, believe it or not. I was desperate.

I started screaming out of control at York Finch emergency. I said, "I lied the first time, I am going to tell the truth." My behaviour that morning was bizarre. Pretending was my only hope to get some attention. But now I was losing my mind. Rubbing my chest, I jumped off the stretcher screaming, "I am having a heart attack." There was a sharp pain in my heart. The pain sent me to the floor. I got up and ran down the hall to a door that said Canadian Mental Health. I became more hysterical and out of control with my heart racing.

Doctor Cooper didn't want to admit me back into York Finch. I heard him say, "I don't want Gladstone here. Does he think that this is a hotel?" I desperately needed some help. There were many fears in my life. I was a troubled young man. However, Doctor Cooper and some of the staff members were insensitive, "We don't want to listen to your physical complaints."

Doctor Jonathan admitted me reluctantly. It took forever for him to see me. He prescribed Mellaril to calm me down. My vision was blurred from the medication. He kept telling me, "You're the healthiest one on the ward." He had me working outside of the hospital. I was cleaning a shopping mall at nights, and my boss would drive me back to the hospital in the mornings. It was difficult working with psychiatric medication in my system. I was frustrating everyone at the job-site for being to slow. Very soon, I was fired.

Doctor Jonathan and Doctor Cooper were insensitive, especially Doctor Jonathan. It was very difficult to communicate my thoughts with them. The psychiatrist was making life more difficult for me.

Doctor Jonathan didn't want to talk about anything physical. He represented himself like a know-it-all. He would quickly move away from me when at times I wanted to talk about my body. He would say, "That's psychological," over and over again. I was obsessed with my body too much. I got frustrated and lashed out in verbal anger. It got very unpleasant on the ward. I was telling the truth about my heart.

York Finch Hospital was for short-term help, and that was my second time around. It was time for another discharge. I ended up living with Aunt Doris again but for a short time. Somehow, later on I was back living with my mother but I can't remember how that happened.

I ran back to the hospital with a bottle of pills in my hand. I was in a severe emotional state and I wanted to commit suicide, but I was really looking for attention. I was desperate. Dominic, a former classmate from high school, saw me outside the hospital with the bottle of pills. I told him, "I am going to kill myself." He said, "I thought about doing the same thing, you know. I had family problems and a bleeding ulcer, but Gladstone I had to live on." He tried to take the pills from me while dragging me into emergency at York Finch. Dominic had a good heart.

The nurse in emergency said to me. "Get out of Toronto." I was telling her that there was no love in my life. At the same time, I was exhausted, and my bizarre behaviour was annoying the nurse. Also, I became very anxious with my heart racing.

My mother had to call an ambulance from home when I became hysterical. At my uncle's house, my heart started to race and I ran out of the house and into the street. Aunt Elaine came outside and saw me lying down on my back in the middle of the street. I was rubbing my chest continuously. No one knew why my behaviour was so unusual.

I was taken to the hospital many times but there were no answers. My Aunt Gwyneth came to the hospital to see me and I told her that I was going to kill myself. She said, "No, you will bring grief to the family." Before she left, she gave me a ten-dollar bill. She did care but nevertheless I felt isolated from my family.

I was never given the proper love from my parents. It was difficult for me to live in this world. I was young when my father ruined everything in the beginning.

CHAPTER 9

York Finch had had enough of my bizarre behaviour. So I was transferred to the infamous Queen Street Mental Hospital. Nothing there was more interesting than Wayne Farr. "Hi, my name is Wayne Farr, from Montreal, brother." Wayne Farr was an awkward-looking black man. And he kept calling me brother and wouldn't stop talking. He would smile and giggle with himself while playing with his hair. The staff members paid no attention to him. Wayne was older than me, and he had brain damage.

I was too preoccupied with my heart and thoughts of dying. Queen Street was a miserable place in 1979. Queen Street was not the place for rehabilitation. The patients were suffering with their medication. They were pacing back and forth in a jail-like atmosphere; there was no place to go. They were robots. It was a terrible scene.

It was hard to concentrate with my mind so far away. I was angry that my father abandoned me in London, England. The significance of that time in London would not soon go away. The doctor was telling me that I was confused. At the same time, my family was afraid of me.

I was diagnosed with schizophrenia. Even though my heart was racing, it was not a heart problem. I thought my head was caving in. My mind was out in space. The chemicals in my medication were tough on the body. Psychiatric treatment in 1979 was survival of the fittest.

Haldol was a pathetic psychiatric drug. The drug was causing weakness to my body. I was always sleepy, and I had a slur in my speech and blurred vision. My heart was still racing at times. However, the staff members did not want to listen to me.

I was physically fine but something physical did happen to my heart that frightening night in my apartment. Psychiatrists love prescribing medication for everything. The psychiatrists were part of the problem. Many times I thought I was going to die.

I was depressed, and my family members were scattering. I was involved in a lot of psychiatric admissions. Also, my heart was acting up, and the summer had just started. It was difficult to cope with my anxiety attacks. At the same time, I had difficulty sleeping with Haldol in my body. My head was ready to explode. I was weak and stressed out with no place to go.

They said that I had an imagined heart condition. The psychologist had mathematical gadgets to read. Doctor Jonathan said, "It's psychological". But at Queen Street, the psychological tests were not taken seriously. Doctor Mandelman's diagnosis was, "Hypochondria, severe anxiety state and simple schizophrenia."

Anyway, I didn't have a place to live when I got to Queen Street Mental Hospital. I had $70 to my name. Still, the doctor didn't want to admit me but I had no place else to go. The doctor admitted me overnight and then arranged for welfare and a boarding-house room the next morning.

I didn't want to stay after I saw the ward at Queen Street. It was nasty. The condition of some of the patients was disgusting.

Queen Street Hospital was a real crazy house. Beverly was a strange-looking black woman in pajamas. She was smiling with herself. It didn't take long before I started to do the same.

I saw a fat woman wearing lots of makeup that made her look ugly. She was pacing the floor carrying a purse with her head down staring at the floor.

Ethel Harvey, the old woman, was sitting in a wheelchair crying out, "nurse, nurse" every minute.

Robin Ball, a young boy, kept saying, "Sorry, excuse me," continuously while trying to get into the nursing office. He was annoying.

Edith Romanchuck would scream out, "Edgar, Edgar you black beast."

There was a large psychiatric nurse with one eye sitting in a chair. The nurse looked like a cartoon character.

I was a tall black man with a thick afro, shabbily dressed, carrying clothes around in a shopping bag. I fit right in. I paced around with my hand rubbing my chest all the time.

The psychologist did intelligence testing when I was weary and out-of-shape. It was difficult talking with a slurred tongue. He told me, "Your vocabulary is poor and intelligence is below normal."

I was on the street crying out for help. They didn't want to listen to me anymore. I tried to tell them who I was. Anyway, Uncle Richard brought me back to Queen Street. I had left the hospital after I met with Doctor Mandelman. Something strange happened when I was in my uncle's car with his mother. He belched and continued to belch and said, "You hungry?" still belching. Uncle Richard was under a lot of stress with me being around so much. He had three children to look after.

I was admitted to Northern Four, a section of Queen Street, for an assessment. Everything was complicated, but I was cooperative.

My physical exam showed nothing but I had many physical complaints. I thought my brain was moving around in my head. I was thinking too much about nothing and it was difficult to concentrate. My attention span was short and I had a lot of bizarre thoughts.

Doctor Nundy was the psychiatrist who did the interview. She said that I said I was faking. Sometimes I would say some things that were off the wall like, "I am going to die." When I tried to talk to her she would say, "Talk to your therapist." Doctor Nundy was not thoughtful.

It was repetitive and dull in group therapy. For me, it was uncomfortable sitting there listening to other patients. Robin Ball and Ethel Harvey's behaviour was so odd at an awkward time.

Modecate was another terrible psychiatric drug that was destroying my brain cells. Still, the hospital was the only safe place to be. My mental health was the most important thing. The medication was causing me to have too much saliva in my month. I would refuse to take the medication at times. It was difficult to socialize being weary and sedated in the day. I was suffering in that atmosphere and it was hard to get some understanding from many of the staff members.

Doctor Nunday was insulting at times, "You're lazy," she did say to me. She was giving me a complex. The doctor was full of herself. She had a problem with my personality.

I wanted to be a baseball player by 1979. I was very anxious and worried about death, and I continued to have chest pains even though it was not a heart attack. I was in deep thought most of the time. There was no affection from my parents from the beginning.

CHAPTER 10

I was at Uncle Richard's for the weekend, and it was not a good scene. My family was afraid of me. My uncle became frustrated with my behaviour and he said, "Is Gladstone back here again? I want him to sleep outside." He was tired of me being around so often. My memory remains clear at that point.

Off I went with a bag of clothes and little money. In my heart I knew that I would be on the streets. It was not a happy time. I walked down the hill to the bus stop. My uncle's house was at the top of the road. At the bottom of the road, I sat in the mud by the bus shelter. I began thinking about my sister and our horrible time in London, England and how the wall ball games with Charlie were over.

The bus stopped and I jumped on. I had no idea where I was going. The passengers were staring at a filthy young man. The bus driver kept saying, "You want to get off here."

The bus was going around and around, and the driver was talking in an unusual way, "You want to get off here" continuously. He wanted me off the bus and so did the passengers. I didn't know what was happening. Finally I got off the bus.

I walked into a variety store and bought an ice-cream sandwich. I was hungry. The neighbourhood had beautiful houses. Walking down the hill I saw a man looking at me from behind a pillar from a church. He was looking out the window suspiciously. The temperature was very hot and the sun was beaming down on my head.

The doctors said that I was hallucinating and insane. This strange episode in my life did happen. The streets were full of men circulating around beautiful women. I was behaving like Jimmy Piersall in Fear Strikes Out. Jimmy was a true Boston Red Sox.

The flowers were beautiful in the yard. The landscaping was perfect in that well-designed neighbourhood filled with beautiful mansions. It was like theatre in that neighbourhood. The women were gorgeous but I was out of place.

It was getting dark and I was still walking the streets. Young people were bothering one another on the sidewalk. I was losing my mind and I was still carrying a bag of clothes. My head was in another world. That night, many young people were walking up and down the street.

In the dark there was an old man sitting on a stone. He started talking, "Go to the back of the building. There is a lot of action back there." It was dark so I did not go. I heard voices along with laughter from the back. Anyway, I left the old man sitting on a stone.

I remember running onto a waiting bus. The bus driver was turning the steering wheel round and round and he kept saying, "You want to get off here." His eyes were wide open and bright-like and ready to pop out. I was standing at the front looking back at this woman. Her eyes were wide open and ready to pop out. They were staring and it was hypnotic. It was still dark and I wanted to stay on the bus, but I was dragged off by two police officers. I reacted violently towards them for putting me on the street.

Again, I was on the street near a subway station. I walked in and spent the night. I was on the subway when a strange man came over who was looking to sell drugs. He was talking a lot of nonsense with his yellow teeth showing. His appearance was awful and he wouldn't stop talking. The drug dealer looked familiar. He tried to get me to snort some cocaine at a nightclub downtown when I was in college. Eventually, the subway conductor escorted me out of the subway. Still the drug dealer kept following me before disappearing.

It looked like a masquerade party on the streets. The strangers were carrying signs and shouting like it was a demonstration. It was a wild night. They had on unusual costumes in the street. I was sitting with a pimp. He dared me to try and cup a girl. Cup was the street talk for picking up girls. The pimp had a lot of dollar bills in his hand.

This was the moment when I was locked in a room that had no door handles. Inside the room there was a dress with no sleeves lying on the bed and a toilet was to one side. I was alone at a tragic time. I entered the room somehow and I was standing there naked. I had to put on the dress with no sleeves to cover myself. And behind the door staff members were dressed in white and looking through the screen-window. They were laughing and mocking me. The staff members were looking at me from behind the screen-window constantly.

It was difficult trying to understand what was going on in my mind, and the pain in my heart was still there. A staff member in white would open the door to feed me but he stood far away from me. I was eating bread from the floor.

In another room I saw a man banging his head repeatedly against the bar doors and another man was playing with toilet paper. A door was open and I saw a black man running around naked and another man was behind the pillars in glasses and he was watching me. It was insane and I remember being there.

My mouth was dry and I was very thirsty but I had no water to drink. So I flushed the toilet a few times to make sure that the water was clean. Next, I put my hand in the toilet to scoop up some water to drink and I did drink.

I was standing in the room when I heard thunder and lightning and the great voice of God. I started to panic. The thundering and lightning continued. I saw light on the wall. The light was beautiful but the thundering and lightning was scary. I became hysterical while listening to the methodical voice of God, which became part of my heart. I began talking about eternal life with the voice of God. I was afraid. God was in my consciousness. Later, the doctor said that I was psychotic.

My childhood was different but that's another time and place. The world was coming to an end like the time of Noah. I wanted to find lasting peace. I didn't want to die, that was the feeling I had when I had bronchitis.

I became emotional when I heard the voice of God. I wanted to live forever. God remains forever in my heart. The conversation I had with the rumbling voice of God was real and frightening. My body somehow became thinner for a moment. God's voice was loud. The more I became hysterical, the more the voice became louder. The thundering and lightning continued and my mind was in another world. I was crying helplessly.

Still the doctors didn't believe that I heard the rumbling voice of God. The doctor said, "No, you had a psychotic episode." I saw light on the wall. I walk with God and that's permanent. It doesn't matter what the doctors say. I believe that it was the voice of God.

I remember the jail cell and the toilet to one side. The bed was rock-hard. The police officer kept asking me, "Are you hungry? Do you want something to eat?" I was lying on the bed when he brought me a McDonald's meal.

The police had me in the back of the paddy wagon with other captives. It was difficult trying to understand what was happening. Somehow I committed a crime but it did not register in my head. The captives thought I was crazy. I was in a cell by myself. Some of the officers were laughing when I said, "I destroyed my own people."

Outside the jail I heard constant banging and talking. The banging continued and the fear of dying was always on my mind. It was frightening sitting in the back of the police car in handcuffs. They were taunting me on the way back to Queen Street.

A staff member wanted to know why I ran away. She said, "Hi! Welcome back." I was coming down from a great high. The doctor said, "You were hallucinating at the asylum." Right away, I phoned my uncle's house. Sheila, my uncle's sister-in-law, answered the phone. She said, "Where are you? Where did you go?"

CHAPTER 11

The summer was coming to an end. At that time, New York Yankee great, Thurman Munson, died in a plane crash. He was dynamic and the Yankees captain.

I had no idea what was happening to my mind that summer. I thought my uncle had contacted Queen Street to report that I was missing. He did not bring me back that Sunday. Anyway, there was communication between the hospital and the police. The cops broke the law before I was in custody. I had a bench warrant on me and I was to appear in court.

The police were offensive, making derogatory remarks. They knew I was a patient, but they didn't take me back to the hospital. A staff member from Queen Street called 33 Division to find out what they were going to do with me. The cops told the staff member that I was still in custody and I had gone to court and remanded to show cause. I was to be provided with a lawyer. The police were charging me with attempt to break and enter. The arresting officers were Milan and Zaychuk from 33 Division. They were rude by the way they conducted themselves. I remember hearing them say, "attempt to break and enter" several times with laughter.

I was tired from the medication and hungry at the station. The police never talked to me. I was sitting and hoping that my uncle would pick me up. At the same time, I saw my mother's address on a piece of paper.

The attempt to break and enter allegedly happened at E.J.K Real Estate at 1333 Sheppard Avenue East. I was on a bus headed south on Kennedy and Antrim. Sheppard was north on Kennedy. An alarm went off at the North York Medical Arts building. I never heard an alarm.

The police wanted to humiliate me from the beginning. They said I was at the rear of the building and footprints were found on the ground. It was a hot summer and I remember that very well. I knew that the police would take me back to the hospital but I didn't want to go back. The police said I admitted to breaking into three doors because I wanted money and drugs. I was not a drug man.

Sergeant Matheson was prejudiced and so was Milan and Zaychuk. Sergeant Jones wrote a report that said, "He is living at 999 Queen Street and he is single and unemployed." The police were walking around saying, "attempt to break and enter" again and again. I had no previous criminal record.

There was something wrong with my mother's attitude. I did not want to live with her. My mother and uncle had taken me to several doctors. At Saint Michael's Hospital the doctor said, "It's a psychological problem." The police said, "He went to almost all the hospitals in Toronto looking for help." Queen Street was notified and they said that they would take me back if I was released from custody.

The police were wicked. Four police officers tried to take my fingerprints but I didn't let them. They grabbed me to put on the handcuffs and a fight broke out. The cops provoked the incident. Still my fingerprints were never taken. They took my citizenship card. I became violent and uncooperative. They knew what they were doing. I was a mentally ill young man.

Milan and Zaychuk created the whole affair. For instance, there were two different addresses on the police report E.J.K Real Estate 1333 Sheppard Ave. East and E.J.K Real Estate 100 University. Matheson, Smith and Jones did a lot of inappropriate things. The investigating officers were liars.

I had another psychiatric assessment by Doctor Butler. The doctor said, "He is lacking competence and the ability to care for himself, and he has irrational fears about being able to destroy the world and being a rat." I didn't eat or drink at the station. My heart was still pounding. I did need assessment and treatment in a therapeutic setting.

I was grossly psychotic and that's the way it was. Once again, I was standing in a room naked. The staff members were watching from the window. I was in Metfors, a special part of Queen Street. That was the place where I heard the rumbling voice of God in a room that had no door handle. I have never been the same since.

I began to think about the great voice of God and the thunder and lightning. I was angry with the police for taking my citizenship card. I received that card when I was 17. I became very suspicious. Some of them were laughing at me. I was trying to understand why I ran away but it was frustrating. The world was against me. I was frightened of Queen Street.

I thought the doctors were trying to poison me. Many times I didn't want to eat. I was taking Modecate and given Stelazine and Cogentin. However, the medication was not working. I was weak and slow. At times I was given needles. I wanted to leave the hospital out of frustration. I was so drowsy and I had a slurred tongue. Everyday I would lie in my bed having strange thoughts. I tried to run away but there was no place to run.

Doctor Nundy stated, "He is suspicious that the police were hiding and trying to catch him." She was loud most of the time. I was talkative and hyperactive while approaching the staff members. They were not helping me the right way. Many times I was put in pajamas.

Sonny Itzkovitch was the one who helped me emotionally. Sonny was not a doctor or a psychologist. He was my lawyer. He was genuinely concerned about my welfare. He protected me from the police. Something was not right with the police investigation. Sonny never gave up on me. I would phone him from the hospital and he never refused my call.

The summer of 1979 was a long time ago. The hospital was trying to make me well for trial by feeding me with barbaric pills. I had to follow instructions.

At that time, I applied for legal aid. Again, a bench warrant was issued against me in court for not being there. However, Sonny was there to represent me. He was such a good guy. The jail doctor sent a letter to the courts. However, the letter was not reviewed by the judge.

I had to get better. I had ground privileges when I met a security guard. He told me that he experienced some of my symptoms with his heart. He thought that he was having a heart attack but he was never hospitalized even though he took medication. He was surprised that I was in hospital. Doctor Prueter, my medical doctor, voiced the same opinion.

I was given a hospital pass to go to court and the police did pick me up at Admitting. Many at Queen Street thought I was crazy. However, I received legal aid with my lawyer's help.

At that time, Doctor Heather White, a psychologist, was my doctor. She told me that she believed in the police and she trusted them. She was not a good help. There was something about me that she didn't like.

Doctor Prueter was different and practical. He wanted to know why I was in hospital. "You should be out there chasing girls," he would say.

I wanted the doctors to decrease the medication. The pills made me dribble from the mouth. It's not normal for the mouth to dribble. The medication was destroying my body. Benztropine Mesylate was the medication that I was taking by the fall of 1979.

I was tired and they wanted me to work. So I started working in the laundry, sorting out dirty linen. The smell was awful. I was getting very agitated with the smell of the laundry and the medication made things worse. I would show up late and then leave early without telling anyone.

Still I refused to participate in community meetings. I was always sleepy. I was more concerned about my court case. My stability was my major concern.

Doctor Nundy was supposed to leave me a report to take to court, and my lawyer was trying to get the crown to drop the charges. The hospital wanted me to stand trial and so did the police. Doctor White informed the police and my lawyer that there was no report. Doctor White was not qualified to write one. Later Sergeant Matheson offered to notify the

Crown Attorney. They were all in it. It was inconvenient for Doctor Nundy to be out of town. I needed that report to stand a chance. Doctor Nunday was on holidays and my fate was in her hands. My lawyer needed the medical report.

Who was really trying to help me? In admitting I was picked up by two police officers in civilian clothing. It was very uncomfortable being around the police.

Doctor White lied to my mother. Doctor White was a plain ordinary Canadian woman. She had promised my mother that a friend would be allowed to accompany me to court. The hospital should have sent an aid worker with me to court but they didn't. The doctor knew that my mother was strange. My mother twisted her hair a lot. She was in another world. The police had made things worst. I was sure that some of them were prejudiced.

The staff members were too involved in my court proceedings. For instance, Doctor White wrote a confidential psychiatric report to the judge and the contents were not to be revealed. I was considered fit to stand trail. In her opinion I was no longer considered certifiably mentally ill within the meaning of the Mental Health Act, but she said I was in need of ongoing psychiatric care for an indefinite period of time. I was suffering from the psychiatric illness schizophrenia and I needed supervision and medication. She was asking the court to make me available to them so that they can prepare a program for ongoing supervision so that

I would be assessed regularly. They wanted me to continue treatment for another two months as an inpatient. Her modest proposal was for the court to place me on probation with the order to continue treatment in hospital. If I failed to attend treatment then my probation officer would be notified and again I would be brought back before the court. Doctor White had no qualifications to be a Crown Attorney.

At the hospital, I did a lot of psychodrama under the influence of drugs. Ruth, one of the patients, would say to me, "Don't you have any ambition?" Doctor Nundy would shout at me, "Wake up you're too lazy."

In 1979, the judicial system had no black representation. The courts were an oppressive place to be. The representation was all white. The Court officials needed more home training especially the police. The judicial system was so prejudiced in 1979.

Father Black was always on the ward and his look was unusual. Somehow he got into my business. He would accompany me to court a few times but I was always suspicious of the way he would appear. He dressed in all black and his name was Fred Black. I brought back from court the recognizance of bail with three particular conditions and Father Black was with me.

Psychological testing did not solve anything. The test was full of statistics and mathematical jargon. I had known one good psychologist and he was Doctor Keith Floyd from

Ponoka Hospital, Alberta. He was the distant cousin of Pretty Boy Floyd, the notorious gangster.

I was weary, and so often things became tedious. The psychologist wouldn't stop talking. The problem started from the time I met my parents. I knew that Psychiatry had no medication for terrible parents. The hospital wanted me in a stressful situation that made me very anxious.

Anyway, Sonny Itzkovitch was there for me. He went before the judge and the matter was remanded to set a trail date. He spoke to Sergeant Matheson and the Crown Attorney again to consider dropping the charge. Sonny had written a letter to Doctor Nundy asking for help but she was no help. He was advised that if a letter was presented to the Crown Attorney indicating that the criminal charge against me was affecting my therapy and mental health that he, the Crown, may withdraw the charge. The letter must indicate that I was in the care of the hospital when the offence occurred and whether I was able to commit a criminal act at that time. If the letter does not convince the crown attorney to withdraw the charge, then a trail date would be set. He went a little further in wanting the letter to indicate what effect a trail might have on my mental health. Sonny knew that I was innocent from the beginning. He was very respectful and too good to be true.

At that time, I was trying my best to get fired from the laundry. I put my foot under the machine wheel and by doing so everything was shut down but I jammed my foot. The laundry was a nasty place to work. Doctor Prueter looked at my foot. However, it wasn't the smartest thing to do. "Are you still here? You should be out there chasing girls. Why are you here?" the doctor would say. I still got fired, however.

I didn't want to be the next Wayne Farr. He was never going to get out of Queen Street.

Finally, Doctor Nundy did write a letter to the Crown but it wasn't convincing. The Crown did not feel sure about the content of her letter and if I was well enough. The Crown was worried that if I was released I might get myself in trouble.

Sonny Itzkovitch was the one who saved me from the Crown. Sure, the police knew that I was an inpatient when they picked me up on the street, and for sure the hospital was getting me ready for trail, which was despicably on their part. My back was against the ropes. I was suspicious of everyone including my own family members. The police took liberties of me with help from Doctor White, but Sonny was fighting for me.

I wasn't eating properly and my medication was increased. They kept me sedated and slow, and it was hard to concentrate. It was a difficult task trying to pay attention. I became emotional when I was traveling back and forth to court with the police. Doctor Nundy said, "He is psychotic under the least amount of stress." It was a stressful and painful time for me.

I was back in court with my lawyer before the judge, at which time the matter was put over for another date. The Crown Attorney would withdraw the charge of attempt to break and enter if at that time there was another letter from Queen Street saying that I received treatment and was well. The Crown wanted me to suffer for another three months with the hospital providing me with the treatment that I require. The process went on and on. My situation was so provoking, and the other patients were getting on my nerves especially Ethel Harvey.

Sonny Itzkovitch gave me hope. My family was not there for me when I was in Queen Street mental hospital. The legal problems had the most effect on me. At times, I was angry and frustrated. Anyhow, Doctor White was trying to set me up with day care for another three months. Constantly, I was late for group therapy on purpose. Again, Father Black was there to escort me to court. He was looking over my shoulder. At times, he displayed a good sense of humor. He was much better than a staff member. I had faith that my lawyer would come through for me. Doctor White was detrimental to my court case.

I would smile with myself when I was high on drugs. And I was obnoxious and aggressive with others. Psychiatric medication was the problem. It was very difficult to keep still. I was agitated and my mind was wondering. Psychiatry at Queen Street was a terrible experience. I was being treated like a dog in the mental health system.

I remember Queen Street very well, it was like a prison. Queen Street was not the right place for rehabilitation. I was not profiting from treatment. My physical complaints were real and antipsychotic medication created side effects that destroyed my will to get better.

My heart was the problem and my mind was on my heart for which there was no cure. I thought about my heart so much so that it was hard to function. I was harassed by the police and humiliated by a collection of staff members. They wanted me to be like Wayne Farr who had brain damage.

Stelazine was another drug that was making me ill. Spit was always in my mouth. I was so weary. My body was changing for the worst and there was nothing at Queen Street to make me well. I was alone. Life did not stop for me. At will, they were giving me a Modecate injection. My parents did not want to do interviews with the doctors. There was a lot of resistance from my family. The staff members would threaten to call the courts to revoke my bail order if I didn't take the injections.

Time passed and finally the charges were dropped. It was Father Black who drove me to court along with my father and that's hard to believe. When I got back to the hospital I wanted to discharge myself and I did. Wayne Farr was not that fortunate. It was time for me to get out of Queen Street. I was looking through the windows no more.

CHAPTER 12

A few months later, my mother had plans to open a bakery business in Antigua of the West Indies and she wanted me to run the business. After I was discharged, there was nothing to do in Toronto so I decided to go to Antigua for vacation.

When I got off the airplane, I was met by Uncle Eustace, and somehow my luggage was on its way to Trinidad. Later, my uncle made some phone calls. He was the manager of the aircraft.

My uncle had a modest home with four bedrooms, and his wife, June, was a pleasant woman. Antigua was very relaxing and the world was more peaceful. I had the time of my life hanging out at the beaches and the nightclubs with my cousin Ira.

June was the best. She loved me and in my heart I knew that. She was not an actor. My uncle's wife took good care of me. They had seven children together at that time. I respected June for being honest. I went many places with her and it was good. When I got irritable, she listened and she helped me to get over myself. At times, she would get angry and threaten to punish me, and she did when I was out of order. Her best quality was her sense of humour and the way she carried herself. She was the friendliest.

Johnson's Point was a different place; however, my grandmother was the same. The house looked so tiny now with trees in the yard. It was hard to imagine that I was nurtured in that house. My heart was in a different place. Johnson's Point was not my home. The Lynngate feeling was not there.

Miss Cochrane talked about her troubles with her children and she would get angry when talking. It was hard to listen at times. She would stamp her foot on the floor out of anger. "This is bongie house." She loved Uncle Bong the most.

Most mornings I was at the beach. I was alone with my thoughts. From the beach I saw the world for what it was. The ocean was light blue and shallow from where I stood with my footprints in the sand. The coconut trees were blowing to one side and a coconut would fall. I did admire the huge rocks by the seaside, which was perfect. It was warm down by the bay with the seashells. The tides would come in and I did look and it was great. The flow from the current would splash up onto the sand and my footprints would disappear. The timing was perfect and no one could stop what was happening.

The horizon was spread wide across the ocean. The distance was far away but I thought I could get there, but I thought that I might drown even though I could swim. The fear of dying was still there, but I found some inner peace at the beach. Still there was something missing in my world. I jumped into the ocean and started to swim. Water was coming into my mouth but I kept on swimming. I began to think back to 1971 when I was a child hiding in my room at 50 Tourmaline Drive. I remembered all my baseball cards. Roberto Clemente was the glamour of baseball in 1971. I knew that the world would never understand my long and painful journey.

My heart started to race when I got back to shore. I had to go back to Toronto. Antigua was not my home. My life was somewhere in Toronto. I kept on complaining, so eventually my uncle put me on an airplane for Toronto. Johnson's Point was not the same even though my grandmother was there. My vacation was too long and I was glad to be home.

I knocked on the door and my mother said, "Who is it?" She was startled and angry at the same time before opening the door. I was a complete stranger around that woman. I was away for three months. However, she wasn't happy to see me. Her motherly love was not there. No one wanted me around. She was the one who left Denise and me behind. She was never there. I was so depressed while sitting in my room. It was uncomfortable living with no love from my mother.

Right away, my mother wanted to send me to Airdre, Alberta, to live with her brother. "Do you want to go live with Uncle Bong?" Sure, I was glad to here that. My mother was not good to me. She never wanted the responsibility. After I left for Alberta, my mother went to Antigua. I had seen her once since 1980. She said to me in 1999, "It was a mistake to come here." She lost her bakery business. My mother made too many mistakes. At the same time, my sister was living with her boyfriend when I returned from Antigua.

Anyway, I was on my way to Alberta. I was 20 years old with nowhere to live. On the flight I had this uneasy feeling. Travelling back and forth was not a healthy thing. Uncle Bong picked me up from the airport. He had a smile on his face but there was little celebration. Life was so frustrating at that time. My uncle was not close to my mother.

I had no idea what I was doing in Airdre; that was quite embarrassing. I came to Alberta initially to see my relatives from Johnson's Point, but Airdre was not what I expected. Somehow this was not the place to be. I had to get away from my mother, but the atmosphere in Airdre was cloudy at best. I had no plans. Being away from my mother was the best thing. I had a lot of pressure on me from my Uncle Bong, but I wasn't going back to Toronto.

From the beginning, my cousins were like brothers but things were different now. They had stability and a father who ruled with an iron fist. My uncle was not perfect but he did the best he could for Bruce and Les. His love was unconditional even though he made mistakes. He was human.

On the weekends, I went everywhere with my cousins. We stayed out late most of the time. It was one party after another. We still had that bond, which was forever. We were like sailors on a weekend pass. Anyway, my uncle was getting angry at the late nights. He had that obsession with control, which lead to Bruce moving out. Bruce didn't do what his father wanted him to do which was to go to university. It was all fun and games for Les and me. We were chasing women even though Les was in a relationship.

Uncle Bong did put the blame on me. I was a distraction. Les was in college and I was just hanging around. They would put me down like I was the one responsible for all of their problems. They laughed at me too many times in Airdre. Airdre was not fun at all. My uncle was like a steam engine when something went wrong. Anyhow, I had no place else to live but the streets.

Carol, my uncle's wife, was good to me. She said that I was a smart guy. She was a stranger to me like most of the people who were good to me. Finally, I was kicked out of Airdre. It was a big mistake to come to Alberta. Now I was living with Bruce who was so busy and soon to be on his way to Japan.

I was struggling with no job skills and life became frustrating. I had a lot of talent in my heart but that was not enough.

CHAPTER 13

Again, I was in the hospital. I was sick. My uncle's face was full with grief just like the way Miss Cochrane looked when I was suffering with bronchitis. That same time I saw Bruce and Les with their girlfriends at my bedside. History was repeating itself.

The doctors wanted me to take my medication, which I refused but my uncle was there to enforce it. They didn't know my psychiatric past.

I was a patient at the Foothills Hospital psychiatric unit. That was a very confusing period of time. Something spiritual was happening in my life.

My cousin was trying to find the answers. Les told me that he found me at Bruce's home, and I was talking a lot of nonsense while sitting on the bed naked in the dark with bed sheets all around me. He was crying on my shoulders, that I do remember. Later he went to get his father.

Anyhow, I met Doctor Pierce, a psychiatrist from England. He was a polite man with a good dictionary. He told me that he met me suspiciously at the hospital one night but he refused to admit me. Personally, he was too professional.

I was acting out and defiant with my surroundings. I was scaring the other patients with my odd behavior but the staff members were pleasant even though I was difficult. At times, I felt powerful. I was so high it felt like heaven, which was a great feeling. Doctor Pierce would give me a lot of inspiration. "You are a good looking guy, what's your problem?" I was angry about my childhood.

Foothills Hospital was a good hospital. It was better than York Finch. The staff members were friendly and the patients were helpful. I saw no prejudices. Of course there was something wrong with me mentally. I was having a hard time understanding where I was going. Again it was a troubling time with no answers.

I was drawing a lot of pictures late at night. I had plenty of time to think about my awful time in London.

I became too demanding and out of control but I didn't mean to hurt anyone. I was drinking a lot of liquids especially apple juice. I was very thirsty from the side effects of the medication.

The doctors were trying electroshock therapy on me. They were killing my brain cells. I was put to sleep every time. I had no idea if I was going to wake up. My uncle had to sign papers for that treatment.

Shock treatments were for the severely depressed and I was that especially around my family. Shock therapy was not good for the body. From that time, I have had a major problem with acquiring a job skill. My short-term memory was so poor at that time. Shock therapy was a dangerous practice in 1981. The nurse would put a needle in my arm while I lie on a stretcher. They would hold me down and my body would jerk from the shock.

The medication was taking my body to the gutter. My body was weak most of the time. Doctor Pierce said, "You are a manic depressive," and the medication for that was lithium carbonate. The nurse drew blood from me every month to make sure that I was given the right dosage. I was supposed to take that drug for the rest of my life. Lithium was a natural element and so was carbon. It was hard to follow what the doctors were doing.

Anyway, I was high a lot of the times. Doctor Pierce said that I had a "chemical imbalance" in my brain. Psychiatry was not doing a good job on my body. It was the same old thing with psychiatry. Nothing was working. My new psychiatrist was Doctor Lewis. He was a grandfather type of a man. He was also a manic depressive specialist at Foothills. When I was a patient at Queen Street, I was diagnosed with schizophrenia suffering from an anxiety disorder.

Psychiatry was trial and error. The doctors were so complicated. The doctors were educated professionals without an understanding of the human spirit. I had no magic pills on the shelves. Psychiatric drugs were killing my insides. The drugs were knocking me down while distorting the chemicals in my body. They said that I had a chemical imbalance from somewhere; I was sickly when I was suffering from bronchitis as a young boy.

At Foothills, I saw images of people who looked real in front of me when I was high. There was a time when a strange woman took me to pray in the chapel. I humbled myself on the floor by falling down and the feeling was so high. I had to be lifted up off the floor; that was an unusual time in the chapel.

The student nurses at Foothills were there to pass the time away, and sometimes their conversations were worthwhile. I had a lot of pain in my heart from my stay in London, England. The psychiatrist never asked me about my pain or about that terrible time in London. However, the doctors would prescribe medication to calm the situation.

The patients were moving in slow motion and I could see a different world. Was I psychotic? The doctors were not paying attention to what I was saying. They didn't believe me when I told them that I heard the voice of God in a room with no door handles. The doctors said, "You were psychotic."

I would look at the wall and see faces of strangers on the wall. The images would walk down the hall and disappear and no one knew what I was talking about. The voice was real that I heard with the thunder and lightning in the room with no door handles. The psychiatrist would say, "That was psychological," and would want to increase my medication.

Uncle Bong was there for me at Foothills. He was like a staff member. He was worried about me. The nurse told me, "Your uncle says that he loves you." His father abandoned him when he was a young man and he took responsibility for his brother and two sisters. He was tough on them. He was angry with his father, which lead him to become brutal at times. My uncle had choices to make and he made the right ones for his children. They say that he had many faults but so do all of us. I saw tears in his eyes for me. I loved him for what he tried to do for me at Foothills. Where were my parents from the time I was born? Uncle Bong was valiant to take his sons and raise them on his own.

Somehow, I got myself into a lot of trouble and I was discharged on the street. Uncle Bong was upset with Doctor Pierce, but before that Tracy Pope, a friend of mine, gave me an Ankh which is an Egyptian chain which was the symbol for eternal life. She was a special woman from the west who told me, "You have eternal life."

Later that night, I went to Bruce's again but that stay was short. I was out of place and my mind was far away. Bruce was going away on business and he didn't know when he was coming back. I was not working and there was no money for the rent. I was on my own, but before he left Bruce gave me some money.

But somehow I ended up on the streets of Calgary. I was looking for a place to sleep and I did see many strange faces. I was running while at the same time throwing my cousin's money away. It was a very cold night. I was walking down the street and I went into a room and it was dark. I was hallucinating when I saw faces. I couldn't move and the faces were moving in slow motion. I was coming down from a great high. I threw away whatever was in my hand.

Later that night, I was sitting in a restaurant with a man called Ram and I was very hungry. He bought me some breakfast and he offered me a place to stay for the night. Ram had a beautiful house, and from the inside the furniture was polished.

That was also the time when I saw a bizarre horse race on television. A young girl was riding a black horse and she won the race to save her family. She was magnificent at that troubling time. Her family members were not truthful. They didn't believe. The young girl was love. But her relatives were too hard on her.

I remembered Sammy and Mandy, the two girls from Airdre. The girls had me on the run at the park. I had laughter and the understanding of that was great. When I was with my parents, there was no laughter. The girls wanted me to hold their hands and I did. I hugged them and they made me laugh. After that, they took me to the swings. I saw the things I never had. Again, I began to withdraw from the world again. The girls knew something was wrong and I told them the truth. My parents never loved me from the beginning. "We love you," and that's all I ever wanted from my parents.

I would go to the ballpark and teach the kids the game of baseball. I made sure that I gave my heart to all of them and that felt great. The children's heart was the most important thing. I know that they would remember the time when I was like the little girl on the black horse.

I had a book in my hand filled with pictures from the Wild Wild West. At that time, Ram told me that he was going to bed. I was by myself when I took the book and ripped it up into three pieces. I then put each piece under the bedroom doors but I have no idea why I did that. After that, I walked out of the house and into the cold.

Again, I was back in the hospital and it was serious. I started smashing things. I went down to the chapel and took the cross out of anger and brought it to my room. Then I put the cross right beside the picture of the Brown Bomber,

Joe Louis. Joe Louis was the heavyweight champion of the world at the time of deep segregation in America. He was my hero. Anyway, I have no idea why I ran to the chapel to take the cross.

After the commotion, I was given three needles to knock me out and I was sent up north to Ponoka Hospital, Alberta for long-term treatment. I was institutionalized again and I was homeless. I was crying when I was saying goodbye to the Foothills staff members. Some of them were very sad to see me go. In the back of the ambulance, I was unconscious as I travelled to the hospital and it was wintertime.

CHAPTER 14

Doctor Mair was my psychiatrist at Ponoka Mental Hospital and he was wise with a lot of class and understanding. He did not believe that medication was for everyone. His personality was more genuine than the other psychiatrists I knew from Toronto. Ponoka was a safe place to be.

I jumped for joy when I got to Hopewell South, which was a section of Ponoka. I was shaking hands with everyone; I was so high. But that very night, I was put in the side room behind a door with no door handles. I was trying to kick the door down every night. I was making a lot of noise while screaming obscenities at the staff members and patients. I was uncomfortable with that type of confinement. I can still remember the time when I heard thundering with lightning and the great voice of God.

Hopewell was the turning point in my life. Ponoka was more than an institution; it was the place that made me well. Hopewell was the right place to begin to understand who I was. Ponoka was where I grew up and where I found the word of God. I became more responsible for my own behaviour. Some of the patients I met were very interesting. The institution was warm and pleasurable.

Alan Redcalf was a young Cree Indian who would pace the floor constantly moving back and forth in an unorthodox manner. He was a troubled young man who believed in true spirits from the most high. I saw many North American Indians in Ponoka Hospital. They were proud and had great respect for understanding the right to be free. I talked to Frank Crowflag who would pace the floor constantly.

At nights, I was trying to kick the door down from inside the side room. The noise was constant. At one time, they opened the door and four staff members wrestled me to the floor. They were trying to give me a needle to settle me down, but I would get back up and start kicking at the door again before passing out.

I remember Mark Henry, a patient who was laughing, "Shut up! We can't get any sleep." He had a wonderful smile for me every time. It was like heaven when I was around him.

How can I forget Bartley who lives in my heart forever? He would go to the store to buy me sweets and Coca-Cola.

Bartley was the ideal father figure who lifted up my spirit. He made me smile for the right reasons when he took me out for walks. We threw snowballs at each other. While running away, he would laugh. He saw a troubled young man who was struggling to survive. He knew what my problem was and he solved it. He was better than a psychiatrist. Bartley knew that I was deeply hurt, and it was very dark and scary. He knew that my life was very tragic. Mr. Dean and Bartley were two men who cared about me unconditionally. They saw me hurting and held out their hand. They were the good Samaritans.

Ponoka was a mental institution regardless. Some of the patients were constantly talking to themselves but most of them were intelligent. They were not at all crazy; some needed a better world to live in. They came from many different backgrounds. They were the homeless. The world was not made for them and never will be.

David was the one who refused to shake my hand in the beginning. He was very slim and he tried to help me with my behaviour. David was wise and I respected him. He helped me a lot with my anger. At first I did not like him but he was so strong mentally. It was like I was there for an education in spirituality. I wanted to be treated with love.

Harold, the head nurse at Hopewell, was a gentleman and the other staff members were real people. Hopewell South was the right place for me and I was beginning to overcome the fear of dying. A staff member took me to the mall and it was like the Ponderosa. The nurse had a loving attitude. However, they did get angry with me when I acted out, but they knew where I was coming from. I became a better person at Hopewell South. The patients were the ones who molded me into becoming a better human being. I had to control the pain of my childhood.

Luke whose real name was Norman was showering at the same time while I was taking a bath. I had to bow to him when I saw him and he did the same to me. He was in great shape and he said that we were the same while showing me his hands, which were white. My heavenly Father put me in Hopewell.

Ponoka Hospital was like a giant mansion from the outside. Huge keys were used every day to open Hopewell South. My world was changing for the better and Hopewell was where everything happened especially at the party. I was with everyone for the last time. They were all dancing and smiling which was real. It was like yesterday when I asked Mark if I was in heaven, and laughing he said, "Yes." I believed him.

Michael John came to Ponoka with a great smile on his face. He was biblically spiritual. I met him at Foothills and now we were all together Matthew, Mark, Luke and John. It was good.

After the party, they were all leaving one by one. It was unbelievable. I never saw them again at Ponoka except for Bartley who died in the hospital. I loved him for what he did for me. Hopewell was a place where my heart will be always.

I was transferred to Lawn Crest Three, another part of the hospital. It was like a hotel and my room was spotless. George Bakewell was the head nurse and was more like a dad. He was a serious man. He knew who I was and he taught me responsibility. He got me out of bed and made sure that I got to work. George and I were like father and son. He was an honourable man from Western Canada. It was not all fun and games with George.

Anyway, it was time to go back to the real world, which was a tragic place to be. I was going back to a world where there was hope. I was back with a family that I didn't know.

After I was discharged, I went to live at the YMCA cluster in Calgary. And I saw Les. He was studying at the University of Calgary. What a coincidence, he was seeing a girl who was living at the cluster. From there I went to live in an approved home.

It was feeling like London again the way I was bouncing around, and it was time to find my way. The scenery was very hollow in Calgary. It was time to meet my heavenly Father.

At the same time, I was living with Michael John and my girlfriend, Laurie, but things did not work out. I was unhappy in Calgary. My home was somewhere in Toronto.

I was educating myself by reading the classics. I was doing odd jobs and I was still without a job skill. Things were getting out of hand, so I decided to go back to Ponoka with fifty dollars in my hand. I needed to regroup in a world gone wrong. I had no place to live.

Ponoka let me back in and that's how I met Doctor Siad, a North American Indian who worked on Hopewell North. He was a unique doctor. He was my last psychiatrist.

At that time, I had no one whatsoever. I lost four years of my life when I thought I was having a heart attack. I know that I was given eternal life in front of my sister in the spring of 79. The voice of God lives deep in my heart. I understand what it was that night in my apartment. In Johnson's Point, I was an innocent boy and I was loved. Thank God I survived my father. My heart was fine. For the first time I wasn't worried about dying. The truth was that there was nothing in the world worth dying for.

Hopewell North was not like the South; all my friends were long gone. It was time for me to get on with my life. I spent a lot of time in the library reading about the game of baseball and studying black issues. I loved reading about the Negro Leagues of baseball. The books taught me about real life, which was an education. The Negro Leagues taught me the truth about the Constitution of America. It was time to go and serve my heavenly Father.

I went back to Lawn Crest and it was a good stay. George was good to me as always. He wanted to know what was really on my mind but I couldn't tell him the truth. On that day, I knew that I was finished with psychiatry. Somehow I had to stay away from my family. I was on my way to Red Deer to meet my heavenly Father. I was never institutionalized again but I was in a lot of pain and that pain will remain forever. Eternal life was what I found.

THE END